# Building a Better World

# Building a Better World

*Faith at Work for Change in Society*

Malcolm Duncan

continuum

**Continuum**

The Tower Building      80 Maiden Lane

11 York Road      Suite 704

London SE1 7NX      New York, NY 10038

www.continuumbooks.com

First published 2006

British Library Cataloguing-in-Publication Data
A catalogue record for this book is available from the British Library.

ISBN 0 8264 9152 9

Typeset by YHT Ltd, London
Printed and bound by Ashford Colour Press Ltd, Gosport, Hampshire

# Contents

This book is dedicated to three people.

To my wife, Deborah, for her ongoing inspiration, love, godliness and support.

To my mother, Olive Duncan, for her constant belief in me and love.

To the memory of my father, Jackie Duncan, one of the most just men I've ever known. He hated Religion but loved people and longed for an Ireland where people were treated fairly. I'm proud to be his son. My only sadness is that he did not live to read these words.

# Acknowledgements

I am grateful to Carolyn Armitage and the rest of the team at Continuum for their support, encouragement and patience. Your comments, editing suggestions and ruthless eye for detail have made this a better book. Thank you for inviting me to write the book and I look forward to all that lies ahead.

My deep thanks are due to Sarah Stevens for her comments, editing and support. Thank you also for your research and general input. You are an amazing colleague and the best personal assistant I could hope for. Thank you also to Ian Livett, Caroline Seal and Jonathan and Sue Wilmot for their gracious comments on the manuscript and their helpful additions and suggestions for editing and to Phil Andrew for his prayers and helpful conversations. I am sure that you have made this a better book and I know that the things that you do with your lives build a better world.

Thank you to Steve Chalke and Joy Madeiros for their help, support, encouragement and inspiration. It is a privilege to work with two such gifted and passionate people. I learn so much from both of you, words cannot express how deeply I respect you both. Thank you also to Steve for the foreword to the book. I appreciate it in the midst of a very busy schedule.

Thanks should also go to the whole team at Faithworks and Oasis for their care, support and willingness to listen to my ideas and critique them. Also to Katherine Brenchley, Janet Church, Froukje Cradock, Mark Dibden, Judith Doel, Jonathan Dutton, Simon Hall, Phil Hoyle, Virginia Luckett, Barnaby Perkins, Jill Rowe, Jenny Seal, Dave Steell, Dave Vann, Zoe Wallis and the rest of the crew, my thanks and appreciation for your help, support and prayers.

I also want to thank the thousands of people who have heard me speaking about these issues in the past six months. They come from

# Acknowledgements

all around the UK and beyond. For those I met and those I talked to via the web, thank you for your prayers, your stories and your encouragements. Thank you to those who have committed to praying for me through the months of writing. A special thank you to Jon and Jill Shergold for their friendship, support, love and encouragement. Our lives are enriched by you. Thanks are also due to Rob and Sheila Hurley and Tim and Karen Howells. It is a privilege to have worked alongside you all.

To the many, many thousands of people who make up the Faithworks Movement, I trust you will know encouragement and strength through these words. You inspire me. In a million ways, noticed and unnoticed, you are changing the face of Britain and the world. God inhabits every act of kindness and is using you to bring about the transformation we all long to see. A thank you is not enough. It is a privilege to lead this movement forward.

Lastly I am exceptionally grateful to my wife, Deborah, and my four children, Matthew, Benjamin, Anna and Riodhna. My gratitude is also due to Marie Masterman – an added bonus in our family. Their love, support and encouragement keeps me going and without them my life would be so much less than what it is. Each of them put up with a lot to make this book possible. In the midst of a hectic schedule leading Faithworks, they patiently allowed me extra time to write, to think and to pray. Deborah's partnership in life and the whole of what God has called us to do together amazes me constantly. Her thoughtful and provoking comments about the book have made it so much richer.

# Foreword

'The world is changed. I feel it in the water. I feel it in the earth. I smell it in the air,' announced Galadriel the elf as she narrated the prologue to the movie adaptation of Tolkien's *The Fellowship of the Ring*. If the question of spirituality ever went away, it's back – big time. Just last week I picked up a copy of *Newsweek International* in Geneva Airport. Sprawled across its front page was a one-word headline: 'Faith'. Underneath sat a strapline which announced boldly, 'The most important issue in the world'.

Everyone lives by faith. Some choose, on the evidence of the world around them, as they see it, to believe that God exists; some to believe that God does not exist. But each and every one of us, either knowingly or unthinkingly, lives by faith – even if it is only faith in ourselves. Some months ago I took part in a public debate about the nature of faith with Polly Toynbee, the UK-based, secular humanist journalist. Her stance was clear. Faith should be banned from public life – it should play no part in the shaping of our society or corporate life. According to Polly, faith is a private thing and should stay that way. My view is different. In fact, to be honest, sometimes I wish that the word 'faith' could take a holiday and force us all to use the term 'worldview' instead. Secular humanism, Polly's chosen belief system, the view that there is no God; that we are here on our own; that the universe is impersonal rather than personal; that we are the product of time and chance rather than a creator and design, is as subjective as any other. The idea that atheism is built around objective truth and logic, while other 'faith' positions are the result of subjectivity and irrational-ism, is itself subjective and irrational. In the end, everyone – bar none – lives by faith.

A recent central UK government report stated that active Christians were three times more likely than any other group to be involved in the affairs of their communities, beyond their own interests. Why? It's simple – Christian faith works. There is something about it that motivates and inspires. For Christians it's a case of 'no faith, no work'. But this is not some kind of veiled threat – 'give us what we want or we'll take our toys away'. In truth, it's exactly the reverse. Our faith is our engine. It is the reason for all we do and keep doing what we do.

So, in the end, the question is not 'do you live by faith?' The answer to this is always 'yes'. Instead, the real question turns out to be 'is the worldview you put your faith in, worth putting your faith in? Does it work?'

Over the years I have had the opportunity to ask countless people the same question. 'If you could discover what God is doing in the world and then join in, would you be interested?' Here's the surprising thing. No one that I have ever asked has ever said 'no'.

In his best-selling novel *Life After God*, Douglas Coupland freely admits he has no religious background. His book paints a stark, if often humorous, picture of the seemingly purposeless nature of modern life. But it is his closing words that come as the biggest shock: 'Now – here is my secret: I tell it to you with an openness of heart that I doubt I shall ever achieve again, so I pray that you are in a quiet room as you hear these words. My secret is that I need God – that I am sick and can no longer make it alone. I need God to help me give, because I no longer seem to be capable of giving; to help me be kind, as I no longer seem capable of kindness; to help me love, as I seem beyond being able to love.'

When I founded Faithworks back in 2000 I did so because of my conviction that you can never have social change without spiritual renewal, or community transformation without personal regeneration. That is why Christian faith works – and works at every level. Here, in *Building a Better World*, Malcolm Duncan, my friend and now also my colleague both at Oasis and in his role as leader of the Faithworks Movement, explores these powerful, thought-provoking themes and their implications further.

In the course of the book Malcolm makes some key points that anyone committed to justice and to a fairer world would do well to consider. What is the role of faith in general? What are the benefits of Christian faith and spirituality? What does that mean for you and for me as individuals? These are fundamental questions that have a deep impact on our lives and how we relate to other people. Malcolm explores the role of faith in a thought-provoking and challenging way. He takes the reader on a journey from the place of faith in society to the role of faith in each of our lives. He attempts to connect the 'idea' of faith in the world with the 'implications' of faith in our own lives and communities.

His conclusions are challenging. He calls those who live out a Christian spirituality to think about moving from domination to servantheartedness. He suggests that there is a hidden melody in the lives of those who long for justice and a better world. He pleads with the Church to recognize that we cannot change the world on our own. He suggests a different approach to people of other faiths and people of none. At the same time, he challenges those who have dismissed Christian faith as irrelevant to think again. He probes the connection that undoubtedly exists across the values of justice, fairness, compassion and human dignity. He shows that faith is something we need to take seriously. This is not a comfortable read – it is a challenging one, because it asks us to make decisions and to take action. It suggests we *can* and *should* do something.

*Building a Better World* is not an intellectual probing of the issue of faith; it is an applied reflection. It asks something of us as we read it – that we will consider the argument and allow our own attitudes and actions to be shaped and changed by the conclusions that we reach. It is a book that is actually a *conversation*. Conversations are never one way, at least meaningful ones aren't. So in this conversation, we, the readers, are invited to dialogue in our heads and in our hearts with the ideas, arguments and conclusions that Malcolm asserts. As we interact with these things, it's also worth remembering that Malcolm is not just a theorist – he is a practitioner. He is committed to the ideas of partnership and support that he articulates in this book. He is not seeking to make more people believe the same thing as he does. Instead, he is driven by a passion and conviction that Christian faith makes the world a better place when it is lived out.

★

# Foreword

I have no doubt that *Building a Better World* will spark discussion – both within the Christian community and beyond it. I trust that discussion leads to greater understanding of those who share our values but not our worldview. I also hope that the discussion leads to action – to more partnership, greater mutual support and a renewed commitment to make injustice and exclusion things of the past. I know this is both Malcolm's passion, and mine. It can be done.

It is said that William Booth, the founder of the Salvation Army, ended his last ever public address, in London's Royal Albert Hall, on 9 May 1912, with these words:

> While women weep, as they do now, I'll fight;
> While little children go hungry, as they do now, I'll fight;
> While men go to prison, in and out, in and out, as they do now, I'll fight;
> While there is a drunkard left, while there is a poor lost girl upon the streets, while there remains one dark soul without the light of God, I'll fight.
> I'll fight to the very end.

May the same Spirit that inspired William Booth inspire you as you read.

Steve Chalke MBE
Founder of Faithworks, Oasis, Church.co.uk and Parentalk

### 'Building a Better World'

The world is full of people,
Each one is unique and special.
One of them is me
And another one is you.

If we work together
The world will be a team
Love for one another
Together we could be a huge family.

The world is full of people
Each one can love another
This is what we could be ...

If we work together
The world will be a team
Love for one another
Together we could be a huge family.

*By Anna Duncan*
*Aged Eight*

# Introduction

Spirituality is alive and well in the modern world. More and more people are exploring the 'non-material' side of life. At the same time, many are increasingly concerned at the lack of equity and fairness in the world. They look around their own communities and their own nations and wonder why things are as bad as they are. This search for spiritual reality, and a concern for the welfare of others, were particularly evident in the frustration over the way in which George Bush's administration failed the poorest people of New Orleans in the wake of Hurricane Katrina. Somehow the events that followed that natural disaster acted as something of a wake-up call not just in the US, but in the UK and around the world. How could the richest nation in the world treat its own citizens in such a way? What had gone wrong?

The Boxing Day Tsunami of 2004 also acted as a wake-up call. In a world so full of wealth and resources, people wondered why there was no early warning system. The outpouring of aid and support from around the world to help the victims showed that 'compassion fatigue' did not exist. Where there was an understood and perceived need, people would give. The Tsunami unleashed the highest amount of giving in the UK that has ever been witnessed. Yet the depressing reality of HIV and AIDS in the world, and the fact that a child dies every three seconds from a preventable disease, shows that the challenges are not being met. Poverty will never be overcome by government programmes. Marginalization and injustice cannot be defeated through legislation alone. Individuals and local communities must be as much part of the answer as are national programmes and legislation. This new 'localism' inevitably leads to a deeper questioning about the role of motivational factors in changing society. One of those motivational factors must be faith. Where does it fit? Is there a place for it in a

1

modern society and democracy? At what point does faith become a destructive influence and how do governments know where to draw the line between working with those motivated by faith and not working with them?

This is new territory – and new territory demands a new map and a new language. *Building a Better World* is an attempt to show that Christian faith has a positive contribution to make to the world in which we live. It is a simple enterprise that seeks to unpack some of the positive contributions that Christian spirituality can make to a healthy and whole society and community. But it is not aimed just at policy-makers and opinion formers. It is aimed at people who have some kind of 'distant rumour' or imprint of God in their hearts. The book is an introduction to some of the underlying assumptions of Christian faith for those who have little understanding of it. More than that, it is aimed at people who care deeply about the world and have a sense of spiritual awareness, yet at the same time are either put off or confused by the institutional Church. It is not an attempt to explain all of the theological nuances of Christian faith – such a task would take a lot more words than are contained in this book! Nor is it an attempt to convert you, the reader. Rather, it is a dialogue, a conversation with you about what difference Christian faith can make to the world. It is an invitation to think about whether or not your commitment to justice could be matched and strengthened by Christian spirituality.

Something needs to change. The economist, J.K. Galbraith, the author of *The Affluent Society*, led the way in arguing for economic affluence. According to Oliver James, a columnist for the *Guardian*, his death has removed *'the sharpest cartographer of a quarter of a century of misguided navigation'*.[1] The past thirty years created societies, both in the US and the UK, where consumerism, materialism and personal wealth became the measures of success. Yet longer working hours, dual incomes and increased pressure on families and relationships have not made people more content or more

---

1. See the article 'Workaholic consumerism is now a treadmill and a curse' by Oliver James, the *Guardian*, 3 May 2006, p. 28.

fulfilled in their lives. The search is on for a better world. Oliver James writes:

> If your vessel is heading towards a black reef of consumerism-crazed debt, gender rancour and mental illness, just turn the wheel and go in a different direction.[2]

I think that new direction is emerging. I want to explore a spirituality that works to build a better world where justice, compassion and the eradication of poverty are vital. Behind those commitments I think we can find a coherent worldview in Christian faith. But how does someone who is not sure of all aspects of Christian spirituality begin to explore Christian faith in relation to their own lives without a sense of being forced into anything? Can faith *grow* into existence in our lives? Where do such people find safe places to explore and ask questions about Christian spirituality while at the same time avoiding a sense of coercion or expectation that they must 'conform'? I hope this book may provide such a place.

In Part I, I'll explore whether or not faith has a valid place in society at all. In the first chapter I'll unpack the idea that faith is on the agenda in both the USA and the United Kingdom: from pop stars to politicians, people are talking about faith. In Chapter 2, I'll try to challenge the notion that faith is inconsequential. The chapter will suggest that faith should not be held in the backroom of life, but that it is a central motivator and shaper in personal behaviour.

In Part II of the book, I'll unpack a charter for change based on a small but vital section of Jesus' teaching – the Sermon on the Mount – and then, in Chapter 4, I'll explore ten key principles of Christian faith that potentially make a huge contribution to the world.

Finally, Part III explores the personal implications of Christian faith. In Chapter 5, I'll pull out some of the challenges that come from taking the example and life of Jesus Christ seriously. In the last chapter I will explore the questions we might want to consider

2. Ibid.

as we move forward from this point. I try to unpack the implications of working with others and how we might get from where we are to the next part of our journey.

Of course, there is so much more that I could have included here but neither time nor space permitted it. The book is not an attempt to answer every question. My efforts here are offered as part of the answer, not *the* answer. I have the huge privilege of leading Faithworks, which is a Christian Social Movement. Its commitments are clear — the transformation of individuals and communities through Christ. We seek to do that through inspiring, resourcing and equipping local groups of Christ's followers to be intimately involved in their communities. We encourage unconditional service. We also seek to change the way the media and the government think about the Church. Faithworks does not have one single theological point of view nor do we seek to. Instead there are almost 20,000 members and hundreds of partner organizations and groups, each with its own identity and sense of purpose. What we share is a commitment to the marginalized and to an authentic engagement in the world. That being said, the views I express in the course of this book are my own. I am grateful that I have the freedom to express my thoughts and convictions without fear of being caricatured or silenced. That in itself is one of the strengths of Faithworks. The errors and omissions of the work are mine but the strengths of the book belong to many people. For all of those who listened, talked and offered comment, a massive thank you.

Faithworks on its own cannot change the world — no single movement or group can. However, it is my deep conviction that a movement of people committed to social justice and societal transformation can make things better.

As you read these words it is my prayer that you will be encouraged to consider again the contribution of Christian faith to our world and the role it might play in your own life and work.

On 23 June 1963, Martin Luther King Jr addressed a crowd in Detroit and said this: *I submit to you that if a man hasn't found something to die for, then he isn't fit to live.* Many people reading these words are willing to die for the poor and the excluded — for a better world. I am grateful for your inspiration, your work and your commitment. I want to join with you in building a better world and I am convinced that if we can only work together we will achieve so much more than we would if we worked apart. My longing is that together we can discover the spiritual energy and passion that will keep us going and help us see beyond the pain we encounter so often in our own lives and the lives of others.

However deep the struggle, however long the road, there is hope. I am convinced that God is at work in the world through those who are committed to making a difference for the better. The world will be a better place – and your work is helping it become one. I hope that a conversation that begins through these pages will continue as we work shoulder to shoulder to change things. Keep in touch.

Soli Deo Gloria

Malcolm Duncan

(Follow discussion about the issues raised in this book and join the conversation at http://buildingabetterworld.typepad.com).

# Part I

## Does Faith Have a Place?

# Who cares?

1

*Is there a place for Christian faith in the 21st century?*

> Say nothing of my religion. It is known to God and myself alone. Its evidence before the world is to be sought in my life: if it has been honest and dutiful to society the religion which has regulated it cannot be a bad one.[1]

I long for a better world. I want to see a fairer, more just society. I know that the world needs to change. Perhaps you care passionately about the future of the planet and the people who live in it. You're probably one of the people that bought one of the millions of white armbands that were sold to support the Make Poverty History[2] campaign or the sister campaign in the USA, 'ONE'.[3] You think poverty and injustice are wrong and you want to see them stopped. We know things need to change.

I'm also aware of the spiritual side of life – perhaps you are too. You might recognize that life can't be divided up into neat little boxes and tidy compartments. When you think of the ways in which many people ignore the plight of the poor at home and abroad, you probably sympathize with the sentiments of Malvina Reynold's song about suburbia, 'Little Boxes', made famous by Pete Seeger:

---

1. Thomas Jefferson, third President of the US (1743–1826).
2. For more information on this amazing campaign see www.makepovertyhistory.com which will guide you to hundreds of agencies that joined together to make the campaign work.
3. For more information on ONE see www.ONE.org.

Little boxes on the hillside,
Little boxes made of ticky-tacky,
Little boxes, little boxes,
Little boxes, all the same.
There's a green one and a pink one
And a blue one and a yellow one
And they're all made out of ticky-tacky
And they all look just the same.

And the people in the houses
All go to the university,
And they all get put in boxes,
Little boxes, all the same.
And there's doctors and there's lawyers
And business executives,
And they're all made out of ticky-tacky
And they all look just the same.

And they all play on the golf-course,
And drink their Martini dry,
And they all have pretty children,
And the children go to school.
And the children go to summer camp
And then to the university,
And they all get put in boxes
And they all come out the same.

And the boys go into business,
And marry, and raise a family,
And they all get put in boxes,
Little boxes, all the same.
There's a green one and a pink one
And a blue one and a yellow one
And they're all made out of ticky-tacky
And they all look just the same.[4]

4. 'Little Boxes' was written by Malvina Reynolds in 1962 and is a critique of the development of comfortable suburbia. It's probably based on Daly City in California and was made famous by Pete Seeger's performances. I first heard the lyrics through listening to the speaking of an American sociologist called Tony Campolo. He used it to show the downgrading of spiritual values in American and Western life.

You are convinced that there is more to life than what we have and what we do. In a census, you might even describe yourself as a 'spiritual' person. You may have been christened or married in a church, had your children christened or baptized or even had a Christian burial service for a loved one. You would describe yourself as broadly spiritually aware, and if you gave it further thought, you may describe this spiritual awareness as Christian. If so, you are in good company – millions of people round the world have a sense of their own spirituality and some kind of connection (however distant and quiet) with some Christian values. This book is for you. This is because I want to explore the connection between your commitment to a better world and the sense of spirituality you have. It's also because I am convinced that allowing the values of Christ to shape and mould us leads to building a better world. If I were you, though, I would be asking a couple of questions already. Questions like:

- What has Christian faith got to do with building a better world?
- What has Christian faith got to do with me?

These are good questions – ones that demand an answer. The same could and should be asked of any religious worldview. In a sense, religion must prove its worth. Those of us who have a passion to build a better world, with even the slightest echo of spirituality in our lives, will be interested in the answers. If we can work out how the whispering Spirit in our hearts and heads connects with our itching hands to make our world a better place, then our conclusions will have a massive impact on both our attitudes and our actions.

This book is primarily concerned with exploring how *faith in Christ* helps build a better world and what that has to do with us as individuals. This is because I hold convictions that spring from being a follower of Jesus Christ – albeit a tainted, broken, cracked and often failing follower. Jesus is the reason I get up in the morning. While I do not believe that the central purpose of Jesus' coming was to make everyone 'become religious' or 'join the Church' as we understand these terms, it is faith in Christ that has provided me with a spirituality and worldview that works.[5] Jesus remains the shining inspiration at the heart of everything I do and he has the unique allegiance of my heart and my life. As a Christian, and a follower of Christ,[6] I am therefore writing from my own personal conviction and worldview. Others, from within different faiths, will be better placed and more equipped to answer the two central questions of how that faith helps build a better world and what implications their spirituality has on individuals. I look forward to engaging in healthy and constructive dialogue with them. It is important for you to understand, though, that I don't write as a passive onlooker, I write as a follower of Christ. What I'm sure of is this, faith (and, from my point of view, Christian faith), has a lot to say about life! Before we go any further, though, it would be really helpful to start with a brief definition of terms.

## Defining terms

My view of spirituality and faith is not the same as my view of Religion. In fact spirituality and faith are not at all the same as Religion – at least not always. Many people hold the conviction that in a world that is torn apart by violence and division Religion is evil. Their argument would be that in communities that are besieged by problems, 'Religion' and 'spirituality' should be

---

5. This statement will probably have caused some deep consternation amongst some of you. For a fuller unpacking of the idea that Jesus did not primarily come to make everyone a 'Christian', see *Generous Orthodoxy* by Brian McLaren (Grand Rapids: Zondervan, 2004), particularly chapter 17: Why I am Incarnational.
6. I do not think that all Christians follow Christ, despite the fact that they bear his name. We need to remember that 'Christian' was a pejorative nickname given to early followers of Jesus in a town called Antioch in Asia Minor, rather than a title given to his followers by Jesus himself. We also need to bear in mind that early followers of Jesus were actually Jews. They did not need to stop being Jews in order to be followers of Christ. In fact, to have done so would have been a disaster. I wonder if it is likely that some Muslims, Jews, Sikhs, Hindus, etc. are followers of Jesus and remain within their own religion? Mohandas Gandhi is one example of someone from another faith who modelled his life on Christ but did not feel comfortable describing himself as a Christian. I do not believe that all faiths lead to the same God, but I do think that religions share some pretty important values. Understanding that and being willing to learn from one another might be a central way to build a better world.

consigned to history so people can get on with the task of building a better world and learning how to work together. Such a view would contend that there are plenty of other issues that need our time and attention – such as education, housing, justice, overcoming poverty and reducing crime. There are persuasive elements to this view. On the face of it Religion doesn't seem to make much sense of the mess that the world is in. We could go even further. It seems that where Religion is strongest, conflict is often greatest. Coming from Northern Ireland, I can see that. I grew up in a beautiful province full of wonderful people; yet day after day I saw the impact of Religious bigotry and hatred. I was born at the beginning of the 'Troubles' as they are known. Throughout over thirty years of bloodshed and pain, thousands of people lost their lives in a conflict where both sides claimed to have God on their side. The truth is that God is on neither side. There are plenty of people in Northern Ireland and beyond who think that Religion should be ditched both because it is dying *and* because Religion itself leads to conflict, pain and injustice. While I am ashamed and embarrassed by the level of pain and hatred generated by Religious fundamentalism across the world I disagree, however, with the suggestion that spirituality and faith should have no place in public life. That's because I don't think 'Religion', 'spirituality' and 'faith' are the same thing. Understanding the difference between these three is vital for understanding the rest of this book.

BBC Radio Four broadcasts a programme called 'The Moral Maze' in which I have participated on a number of occasions. On the show, two 'witnesses' representing two opposing points of view are interrogated by a panel of four. You can imagine that the discussions become heated and the exchanges very energetic, which I think is fantastic. Recently I was a witness on the programme when the issue of debate was whether or not 'faith' was good for public life in the UK. Hundreds of thousands of people listen to the show, so the pressure is on to make sure you articulate your thoughts clearly and succinctly. It's also broadcast live, which makes it even more interesting.

Throughout the discussion I articulated the view that faith had a vital part to play in any healthy society. At one point in the show I said something like this:

My spirituality is driven by a deep and personal faith in God as revealed in Jesus Christ, however I think Religion and Religious fundamentalism can be very damaging.

A couple of the panellists were baffled! How could I describe myself as having a spirituality, holding a faith but sometimes struggling with Religion? But the three terms refer to very different ideas. Not everyone who is Religious has faith. Not everyone who has faith is Religious. And not every spirituality is worked out through an organized construct called Religion. That probably needs a bit of unpacking! It's important that we use terms that we understand – so let me define what I mean by:

- Religion
- Spirituality
- Faith.

## Religion or Religious fundamentalism

There is no doubt that organized Religious fundamentalism is a curse on our world. Throughout history we have seen extremism devastate communities, and whole people groups. The fact that a whole Christian denomination was formed largely to protect and defend the rights of slave owners must surely be a source of embarrassment for the Church?[7] The atrocities that have been carried out in the name of God have certainly not built a better world. From the Christian crusades of the Dark and Middle Ages to the bombing and murder of innocent people in the name of Allah in the 20th and 21st centuries, Religious fundamentalism has a lot to answer for. I wonder exactly what the difference is between the warped motivation of a 12th-century Christian crusader and a 21st-century Islamic suicide bomber? Both believed that what they were doing was in the name of God, and both were convinced that their actions could somehow 'force' people to

---

7. It is my understanding that one of the primary reasons for the foundation of the Southern Baptist Convention in the USA was to defend and protect the rights of slave owners. I am happy to be corrected if this is an incorrect view.

believe. I do not think it is right, or even possible for that matter, to force people to believe anything.

When I use the word 'Religion' with a capital 'R' I mean what I have just described – organized and structured practices. I actually mean a little more – I mean restrictive and often formulaic approaches to God, the world and our place in it. You'll see as we progress through the book that I have a great deal of time and respect for 'religion' (with a small 'r' which I will unpack as 'spirituality' in a moment) but not so much time or respect for Religion with a capital R. Whether that fundamentalism takes the form of extreme right-wing homophobia condemning gay people and pronouncing that AIDS was God's judgement on the gay community or whether it takes the form of Islamic terrorists attacking and killing other people, I think it's a big problem. I also think that it is this kind of extremism that has resulted in much of the caricature of spirituality. This is because I think most people have equated Religious fundamentalism with religion and spirituality. My sadness is that those who are religious have done little to challenge the caricature.

## Spirituality

Spirituality, on the other hand, is something entirely different. For me, spirituality is much more what *I mean* when I talk about 'religion' (this time with a small 'r'). This is a particular view of the world that believes there is more to life than what we see. It is a series of convictions that pull together to shape how we view the world and everything in it. It starts with a set of foundational convictions about life – its source, its function and its purpose – and leads to a set of behaviours and preferences. Our convictions, our values and our beliefs lie at the centre of our spirituality. In other words, our spirituality is driven and shaped by our faith.[8]

---

8. For a great unpacking of Christian spirituality I recommend you take a look at *Christian Spirituality* by Alistair McGrath (Malden, MA: Blackwell, 1999).

## Faith

For the purpose of this book, faith is understood as the act of believing. As I've already said, my thoughts and ideas are shaped by my Christian faith. For some, their faith is shaped by something or someone else. My point here is not to over-qualify 'faith' but to set it in its context for the rest of our discussion. In other words faith is allegiance to a person, ideal or set of convictions.

The problem with my conversation on 'The Moral Maze' was that the panellists did not have a language that could help them separate out the subtle differences between Religion, spirituality and faith. Most people don't. This is a problem because they then tend to group the three terms together, and by so doing end up in a bit of a mess. By confusing the terms we might judge all Christians by the activity of Christian extremists, or all Muslims by the actions of Islamic fundamentalists. But the vast majority of people across the world hold allegiance to a person or a set of convictions (faith) that shapes their view of God, themselves, others and the world in which they live (spirituality), and they work that out in relationship with others who hold similar views (religion), yet they are not extremists or fundamentalists. They have not suspended their intellect; they have not abandoned the ability to think, to reflect and to debate. They, like me, hold religious convictions that make them better citizens and therefore enrich their worlds.

## Who's saying what – population, pop stars and politicians

Having established a mutual understanding of terms, it's interesting to note that a lot of people are interested in issues of faith today. Public figures seem to be coming out of the woodwork to acknowledge the role of faith in the lives of citizens. There has been a definite change in the way in which faith is viewed in the UK and the USA as well as in many other places around the world. In the 1970s and 1980s it appeared that faith had been relegated to the privacy of our own thoughts and ideas while politics could deal with life. There is perhaps no clearer example of this than when in the late 1980s[9] Margaret Thatcher, then the UK Prime Minister, told the Bishop of Liverpool, David Sheppard, that he should leave politics to the politicians and get on with religion. The ground has significantly shifted since then. Britain is seeking to find a more open and inclusive place for people of faith and their contribution to the public good. In fact, in May 2006 the Church of England published a report entitled *Faithful Cities: A Call to Celebration, Vision, and Justice* from the Commission on Urban Life and Faith that articulates some of the differences between the Britain of the late 1980s and the Britain of the 21st century.

I welcome this shift in view, seeing it as recognition of the simple truth that faith has a healthy and vital role to play in the lives of individuals and in the development and protection of a healthy society. Not everyone welcomes that reality, though. Organizations like the National Secular Society continue to try to portray faith as on the margins of life and call for it to be held to the margins of public discourse. Keith Porteous-Wood of the National Secular Society is one of them:

> The government is increasingly addressing citizens as religious groups, but relatively few people define themselves primarily in such a way.[10]

There is a problem with this view though – it's statistically wrong!

## Population

The 2001 Census[11] collected information about ethnicity and religious identity in the UK. The results show that while the

---

9. 1988, at the launch of the Church of England's crucial report 'Faith and the City', which examined the issue of deprivation and poverty and how Christians could engage in addressing the needs of society. The Commission on Urban Life and Faith's *Faithful Cities: A Call to Celebration, Vision and Justice* is a report published in May 2006 that details the view twenty years on. The findings are striking. Copies are available from www.mph.org.uk.

10. National Secular Society press release entitled 'Government Religion Policies Will Result In Parallel Communities', 1 September 2005. For more information see www.secularism.org.uk.

11. Source: Census, April 2001, Office for National Statistics & Census, April 2001, General Register Office for Scotland. The Census question about religion was voluntary.

British population is more culturally diverse than ever before, identification with Christian faith continues to be one of the largest unifying delineators by far. In Great Britain, 40 million people described their religion as 'Christian'. Furthermore, when the overall statistics are examined a little more closely, it becomes clear that the UK is a diverse and a *spiritualized* society. Britain is home to people from a vast plethora of spiritualities including Muslims, Jews, Sikhs, Hindus and Buddhists.[12]

Somewhat surprisingly, only 15 per cent of the British population reported having no religion at all. These statistics must challenge the idea that spirituality is irrelevant. At the very least, they hardly demonstrate that 'relatively few' people describe themselves as religious in the UK! Given that even Secular Humanism can be seen as religion, this figure would drop even further. What is true for the UK is also true in the USA, where the vast majority of people identify with a 'spirituality' or religion of one kind or another. For example, around 35 per cent[13] of Americans still regularly attend church services compared to just 8.5 per cent in the UK. As we will explore later, the 'Christian' vote in the US has even been identified as the key support that ensured George W. Bush's victory in the last presidential election. Far from religion having become something that is no longer relevant, it is increasingly relevant. At the same time, it is important to remember that many of those who describe themselves as 'spiritual' people would not want to be labelled 'religious'. *Spirituality* and *religion* are not seen as the same thing, because they

12. Majorities of Black people and those from mixed ethnic backgrounds also identified themselves as Christian (71 and 52 per cent respectively). In total there were 815,000 Black Christians and 353,000 Christians from mixed ethnic backgrounds. Among other faiths the largest groups were Pakistani Muslims (686,000) and Indian Hindus (471,000) followed by Indian Sikhs (307,000), Bangladeshi Muslims (261,000) and White Jews (259,000). The Indian group was religiously diverse: 45 per cent of Indians were Hindu, 29 per cent Sikh and a further 13 per cent Muslim. In contrast the Pakistani and Bangladeshi groups were more homogeneous, Muslims accounting for 92 per cent of each ethnic group. Some faith communities were concentrated in particular ethnic groups. For example, 91 per cent of Sikhs were Indian and 97 per cent of Jews described their ethnicity as White. Other faiths were more widely dispersed. Considerable proportions of Buddhists were found in the White, Chinese, Other Asian and Other ethnic groups.

13. This number is declining and I think that the American Christian Churches are going to face a similar process of change and challenge as have the Christian communities in the UK since the Second World War.

are *not the same thing*. The truth is this – organized religion may have waned but spirituality has not. Millions of people identify themselves as part of a religious heritage even when they do not practise religious rituals. To suggest that this does not matter is the equivalent of suggesting that because only 57 per cent of the UK population voted at the last election, the other 43 per cent do not believe in democracy!

## *You are not unusual, but you are unique!*

The vast majority of citizens in the UK and the US consider themselves to have a religious affiliation of one kind or another. Whether or not they are active participants in religious life does not negate the fact that they consider themselves linked to a faith. That means that if you are reading these words with a vague sense of spirituality, an *echo* of spirituality, then you are with the majority, not the minority! It is *normal* for us to have a sense of spirituality, not abnormal. Somehow we need to allow ourselves the opportunity to explore that sense of spirituality rather than ignoring it or treating it as unimportant. There is no doubt that you will have a unique take on the world and on how it should be put right, but there is also no doubt that there is room to explore the spiritual foundations for why you feel that way. Indeed, to explore the side of your character that longs for injustice to be overcome without exploring a worldview that underpins it might even be short-sighted. The connection between spirituality and action is vital if our action is to be sustained over a longer period of time.

It's helpful to understand that you are not alone in exploring your spirituality. Others have acknowledged the need to engage both heart and soul in the search for a better world. Exploring the connection between justice and spirituality is happening all the time. There are thousands of people that could be cited as examples of those exploring the link between spirituality and the way we live, but I want to unpack thoughts from two groups of people – pop stars and politicians.

## Pop stars

Bob Geldof's involvement in trying to eradicate poverty in Africa is well known. From Band Aid in 1984, to Live Aid in 1985 and more recently Live8, Geldof has given masses of time and energy to raising the issues of poverty and injustice. At the time of writing, he is preparing to give an address in Westminster Catholic Cathedral around the issue of faith and society.[14] He is acutely aware of the need to engage *spirituality* in the fight against injustice and poverty. In fact, he has described the realization of the strength of this connection as 'like a light turning on in my head'.[15] Commenting on Geldof's ideas and the deep connection between justice and spirituality, the columnist Madeleine Bunting writes:

> Geldof has astutely blown open a much needed debate: economists and politicians have dominated the agenda of African development for half a century, and look where it's got us. Economic growth is not just about technical knowledge, but also about human behaviour – and that is rooted in beliefs such as what constitutes progress and development. Indeed, what is wealth? These questions are spiritual as much as material in Africa; if we appreciated more of the African understandings of these concepts, we might learn as much from Africa as Africa is expected to learn from the west.[16]

What is true for Geldof of Africa, must surely be true of us as we engage in our societies and communities in the UK and the USA? Politics cannot exclude faith motivation. For it to do so is both to reduce politics and to reduce faith. Such reductionism is a common trait at the moment, but it is one that we must resist.

Bono, the lead singer of the popular rock-band U2, has also

---

14. See www.rcdow.org.uk for more details.
15. See Madeleine Bunting's piece in the *Guardian*, 28 March 2005, entitled 'Where Faith is a Healer' where she suggests that the answers to Africa's problems lie with spirituality rather than with politics.
16. For further details on Madeleine Bunting's interview with Bob Geldof and others see http://yaleglobal.yale.edu/display.article?id=5479.

been very vocal about the connection between building a better world and faith.

> To me, faith in Jesus Christ that is not aligned to social justice – that is not aligned with the poor – it's nothing.[17]

He goes further. For Bono, faith not only *can* lead to action, it *must*. He has repeatedly argued that Christians must engage in issues of injustice and poverty if they are to authentically model their faith. He spoke at the National Prayer Breakfast in Washington DC in February 2006:

> These religious guys were willing to get out in the streets, get their boots dirty, wave the placards, follow their convictions with actions – making it really hard for people like me to keep their distance. It was amazing. I almost started to like these church people.[18]

However, it is interesting to note that Bono struggles with the structure of organized Christian religion like many other committed followers of Jesus Christ. In an article in 2003 he said:

> I'm not so comfortable in the Church, it feels so pious and so unlike the Christ that I read about in the scriptures.[19]

For Bono, it is vital that the Church does respond to the needs of the poor and the marginalized. He sees its future in its willingness to stand on the edge of society with the outcast, the forgotten and the neglected.

> If the Church does not respond to this, the Church will be made irrelevant – millions and millions of lives are being lost to greed,

---

17. Bono, quoted in *Walk On: The Spiritual Journey of U2* by Steven Stockman (Orlando: Relevant Media Group Inc., 2005).
18. Keynote address at the National Prayer Breakfast, 2 February 2006, Washington DC.
19. Bono, quoted in 'Bono's American Prayer', *Christianity Today* 47, no. 3 (2003), by Cathleen Falsani.

to bureaucracy, and to a Church that's been asleep, and it sends me out of my mind with anger.[20]

Lastly, the Black Eyed Peas recorded a song entitled 'Where is the Love' for their 2004 album, *Elephunk*. The lyrics are startlingly forthright as they challenged listeners to think about the society that we are part of. The song climbed high in the charts in both the US and the UK. Its whole message could summarize what I'm trying to say in this chapter.

## UK politicians and heads of state

There is no doubt that the political landscape now has room for dialogue around faith and public life. In the run-up to the 2005 UK general election, which was subsequently won by the Labour party, Faithworks invited those who were the leaders of the three main political parties to address the Church on the issue of the role of faith in the 21st century. All three acknowledged the fact that faith has a positive and healthy role in modern British life. All three spoke positively of the ways in which local communities were changed by the presence and support of different faith groups. Perhaps most interestingly, all three spoke of the need to strengthen the role of faith groups, not remove them. They recognized that faith is good for society.

Charles Kennedy, the former leader of the Liberal Democrat party, clearly grasped the connection between building a better world and the motivation of faith. He said:

What people sometimes fail to acknowledge or recognise is that the focus of most faith-based organisations is more practical and more domestic. It's a matter of battling poverty, here and abroad; or seeking to give our children a decent start – keeping

20. Ibid.

them away from drugs and crime; and at the other end of the lifespan, caring for our elderly and infirm.[21]

Like Iain Duncan-Smith before him,[22] Michael Howard, former leader of the Conservative party, also made it clear that from his point of view the motivation of religious life made an important contribution to a healthy British society:

Religious faith makes a distinctive and vital contribution to Britain's public life and is a force for our well-being.[23]

David Cameron, the present leader of the Conservative party in the UK, also appears committed to exploring the role of the faith sector in the public life of Britain and the provision of services. He has established a key think tank on social exclusion and highlighted his intention to put social inclusion at the heart of his manifesto commitments for the next election. His commitment to the Centre for Social Justice is an encouraging sign of an established link to social justice and recognition of the vital role faith groups play in regenerating the UK.[24]

Tony Blair has become increasingly open to the place of faith in public life as well as to articulating his own Christian faith and how it has motivated him. In the Faithworks lecture of 2005, he said:

I know that people talk a great deal about the decline of religion and the churches in our national life. But in terms of social action and commitment, community by community, it is your revival and adaptation which are striking.[25]

21. Charles Kennedy, Faithworks Lecture, 2005. Further information available from www.faithworks.info.
22. For more detail of the connection between faith and society's well-being in One Nation Conservatism see Iain Duncan-Smith's report *Sixty Million Citizens* available from the Centre for Social Justice, Hawkstone Hall, 1A Kennington Road, London.
23. Michael Howard, Faithworks Lecture, 2005. Further information available from www.faithworks.info.
24. For more information see www.centreforsocialjustice.org.uk.
25. Tony Blair, Faithworks Lecture, 2005. Further information available from www. faithworks.info.

While seven or eight years ago Tony Blair's communications director famously said that New Labour 'did not do God', there seems to have been a shift in thinking. Recently Blair spoke of his own religious convictions and his accountability to God for his decisions in a televised interview with the journalist Michael Parkinson.[26] Not only has Blair recognized the importance of faith in building a better world, but so has the wider UK government. Endorsement of the city academies and schools of religious character have underlined the commitment of the UK government to work with faith communities to regenerate communities.[27] Gordon Brown, the current Chancellor of the Exchequer, has also endorsed the role of faith in improving communities and society at large. Speaking at the National Council for Voluntary Organisations Conference in the UK in 2004, he said:

> Prosperity and improvement must be founded on something more and something greater than harsh organised selfishness: instead a sense of social obligation – often infused with religious values – and a broad moral commitment to civic improvement.[28]

Even Queen Elizabeth II has spoken more openly of her Christian faith in the past few years. It would appear that her annual televised address to the nation at Christmas time has been an important vehicle for her in this regard:

> [Jesus'] great emphasis was to give spirituality a practical purpose.[29]

---

26. For details of the interview and comment on it see http://news.bbc.co.uk/1/hi/uk_politics/4772142.stm. For the record, I think Tony Blair has been misquoted badly by the press and media. He actually talked about being accountable to God for his decision to go to war in Iraq, not that God had told him to go to war.
27. There is a target of 200 city academies in the UK in the next five to seven years. Oasis Trust, the leading partner of Faithworks, is currently planning to build and run six of these academies as schools of religious character.
28. Gordon Brown, keynote speech at the NCVO annual conference 2004. For further details see www.ncvo-vol.org.uk.
29. Queen Elizabeth II, Christmas message, 2000.

There may be an instinct in all of us to help those in distress, but in many cases I believe this has been inspired by religious faith.[30]

While there is still a reticence in the United Kingdom to wear our faith on our sleeves, there is a greater degree of openness to acknowledge and explore the link between faith and society than ever before. This is an opportunity that cannot be missed.[31] The UK is not in the place of Continental Europe where faith has very little opportunity to speak in the public square, nor is it in the place of the USA, as we will see in a moment, where politicians are much more open about their faith. However, there is much to learn from the UK's approach. There is not the wholesale endorsement of one particular party by the Church in the UK, and Christian faith is perceived to be more progressive in Great Britain than it often is in the USA, although the right-wing domination of the Religious (with a capital R!) agenda in the United States is beginning to change.

## American politicians

The most notable political commentator on faith and society in the USA is George Bush. Criticized for many of his comments and for the narrowing of the moral agenda, Bush should also be acknowledged for being open about his own faith and its motivation for his work. He has commented that he knows the power of faith to change lives, because it has changed his own life.[32]

---

30. Queen Elizabeth II, Christmas message, 2005.
31. Faithworks is committed to exploring how this opportunity to discuss the role of faith in public life can be understood and built upon. We are committed to working with government and other faith groups within an approach that we have labelled 'Distinctive Faith'. This area of our work is being spearheaded by Joy Madeiros. For more information please see the Faithworks website – www.faithworks.info.
32. 'Faith changes lives. I know, because faith has changed mine', George W. Bush, *A Charge To Keep*, co-written with Karen Hughes (New York: William Morrow, 1999), p.136.

At the State of the Union Address in 2005, Bush acknowledged the trickiness of the relationship between society and faith, but argued that the link was clear:

> Our great responsibility to our children and grandchildren is to honor and to pass along the values that sustain a free society. So many of my generation, after a long journey, have come home to family and faith, and are determined to bring up responsible, moral children. Government is not the source of these values, but government should never undermine them.[33]

Introducing Bono's keynote address at the National Prayer Breakfast in Washington in 2006, Bush highlighted the example of Jesus to millions of Americans as an inspiration for improving the well-being and health of their society:

> What I've found in our country, that whatever our faith, millions of Americans answer the universal call to love your neighbor just like you'd like to be loved yourself.[34]

Bush does not have a monopoly on endorsing the role of faith in society in the USA. The defeated Democrat presidential candidate, Al Gore, is also committed to the role of faith in public life.

> Americans' volunteer work has doubled in 20 years, even as more women – the traditional mainstay of volunteer groups – have moved into the workplace. [Americans'] hunger for goodness manifests itself in a newly vigorous grassroots movement tied to non-profit institutions, many of them faith-based & values-based organizations. I have seen the transformative power of faith-based approaches through the national coalition I have led to help people move from welfare to work – the Coalition to Sustain Success.[35]

33. George W. Bush, State of the Union Address, 2 February 2005.
34. George W. Bush, welcome to the National Prayer Breakfast, 2 February 2006, Washington DC.
35. Speech made by Al Gore on Faith-Based Organizations, Atlanta, GA, 24 May 1999. See www.ontheissues.org for more details.

John Kerry, the defeated presidential candidate for the Democrats in the 2004 election, also spoke openly of his own faith and convictions:

> My faith, and the faith I have seen in the lives of so many Americans, also teaches me that, 'Whatever you do to the least of these, you do unto me.' That means we have a moral obligation to one another, to the forgotten, and to those who live in the shadows. This is a moral obligation at the heart of all our great religious traditions.[36]

## Where does that leave us?

People, pop stars and politicians all point to the fact that faith has a place in public life. They say something more, though. They make it clear that the motivation to build a better world can often be deeply connected to the way in which we view that world. If the vast majority of people in the UK and the USA acknowledge some kind of faith affiliation or spiritual motivation, then it is vitally important to explore what that connection might mean for our individual daily lives, our communities, and our world. In fact exploring the connection is one of the *most* important things for us to do. Separating our actions from our motivations has never worked, because it doesn't make sense. Trying to build a better world without making sure the foundations are right is like building on sand. Getting our foundations right means we will build on solid, reliable ground. Exploring our foundations must be one of the most important undertakings of our lives. It is a journey we must make.

This journey may not be a comfortable one for you or for me. We may disagree on the way. You may find that some of your misconceptions are challenged or your ideas shaken a little. I hope mine are too. I'm not interested in converting you. I'm not

---

36. Speech at the Broward Center for the Performing Arts, 24 October 2004. See www.beliefnet.com for more details.

interested in coercing you. I'm not even interested in just persuading you. What I do want to do is to help you to explore how the passions of your life might just coincide with the Giver of Life himself. It might just be that your longing for a better world is about to be given a greater depth and meaning than you realized.

Too often the Church has been unable to celebrate the spirituality that is connecting people to issues of justice and fairness. Christian spirituality is not a one-size-fits-all mentality. Such a spirituality actually celebrates diversity and difference. It welcomes a spectrum of people and ideas whilst celebrating common principles and commitments. The challenge has been that Christian faith has not always communicated that reality. Things are changing, though! Those who do hold Christian convictions in politics are beginning to be more open about them, with politicians increasingly recognizing the need to engage with faith groups more effectively. Campaigns such as Make Poverty History, ONE and the Jubilee Debt Campaign are helping people who share common values to work together, even if they do not share the same faith. Followers of Christ are becoming more and more involved in such activity. Social activists are also becoming more open about the motivation of their faith. The Faithworks Movement in the UK is made up of thousands of projects that are aimed at helping communities. The projects are run by people who are motivated by their Christian faith. In the US, the growth and development of events such as Urbana and the growth of churches like Redeemer in New York show that followers of Christ are becoming increasingly confident about allowing their faith motivation to propel them toward community engagement. It is clear that political activism, social engagement and community development are all areas where those who hold to a Christian spirituality are exploring new relationships and partnerships with people who hold similar commitments to justice and compassion.

It might just be possible that those people with the desire to overcome injustice, to obliterate poverty and to see needless deprivation, violence and prejudice removed have a perfect hero in Jesus Christ. It might also be possible that values such as respect, trust and hope are universal values which traverse cultures, communities and even religions.[37] Rather than shouting at those who do not share my faith, wouldn't it be better to enter into a dialogue with them, perhaps with you, about a Christian spirituality that undergirds our passion and commitment to build a better world? Our Christian spirituality might also be one that can undergird your own passion and commitment. It may even be the spirituality that you have been looking for. In North America and in the UK there is willingness and openness to explore spirituality and its connectedness to social change in a way that has perhaps never existed before. You and I are part of a culture that wants to question, wants to delve, wants to explore. So why not explore together here?

What if your passion for change in the world was given to you by God? What if your passion for the planet has been given to you by the One who made it? What if you can see how to use it most effectively in the life of Jesus? What if your understanding of Christian spirituality has been coloured by your understanding of Religion (with a capital R) rather than by the example and person of Jesus? What if the energy to keep going when everything in you tells you to stop can be discovered in being connected to God, through Christ? What if Christianity has a manifesto, which, if understood and applied, would create the fairest, most inclusive society and world imaginable?

## What if Christian faith works?

At the heart of the understanding of my own faith and therefore at the heart of my spirituality there are three deep convictions. Those convictions shape all that I do. The first is that Jesus Christ is the greatest example of a human being I have ever encountered – he is my hero. His life is a masterpiece of mercy, a celebration of compassion and a symphony of justice. He is the artist of inclusion.

37. For two fantastic books on values see *Hope, Respect and Trust* by Joel Edwards (Milton Keynes: Authentic, 2004) and *Trust: A Radical Manifesto* by Steve Chalke (Milton Keynes: Authentic, 2004).

I see in him the traits that I want to have. I find in him not only inspiration, but hope. When I am tired and think the job cannot be done, I think of him and find energy again. When I become angry and want to lash out, I find patience and resolve through thinking about him. When I complain of the cost of building a better world and wonder whether it is worth it I think of the price that he paid and the commitment he showed and I am strengthened to keep going. I think we all need heroes. I have a number of them – Gandhi, Martin Luther King, Florence Nightingale, William Booth, Lord Shaftesbury, Mary Slessor.[38] But they all had a hero that I share – Jesus. We'll look more at this in Chapter 5. As a follower of Christ, I do not see him as one of a number of options. The crunch for me is that he is both a human being and God in the flesh. It is this central and unique assertion that makes me not just a follower of Jesus but someone who worships him.[39]

The second conviction is that Jesus' teaching and manifesto is as world-changing now as it has ever been. We will look at this in more detail in Chapters 4 and 5. Followers of Christ have something powerful and positive to say about the world in which we live and the communities of which we are a part. When disciples of Jesus are caricatured as people who rant and wail in a tirade against the things they do not like it is an offence to God and should be an offence to those of us who seek to follow Christ. The sadness is that such a caricature is often true – I want to begin to address that imbalance.

Thirdly, I am motivated by hope, not by cynicism. It is easy to throw our heads up in despair and to complain. It's a bit like being in opposition instead of government. The former means we can say how things should be, the latter has to get on with the job of governing. I think every single person has a responsibility to be

38. Mary Slessor was a missionary from Dundee. She lived a remarkable life and is probably less well known than many other people I will mention in this book. Her courage, conviction and commitment are an inspiration to me.

39. There are many people who see Jesus as a great example, a fantastic moral teacher or an inspiration but cannot or do not recognize him as God. It is this central assertion that lies at the heart of Christian faith – the belief that Jesus was both a human being and God made flesh. It is also this belief that puts in perspective the amazing examples of love, grace, acceptance and inclusion that are displayed as traits of God's character *through* the whole life and example of Christ.

part of the answer, not part of the problem. We'll explore that in the last section of this book. What kind of society do we want to be a part of and what kind of world do we want our children to grow up in?

You may have been singing the lyrics of a song about a better world for a long time, yet be unsure of the tune. Politics has not provided the notes that you need, nor has philosophy. Self-reliance has caused you to sing off-key too many times; looking to others to sort out the world has not always led to the greatest harmony and your understanding of human nature has perhaps not provided the right key in which to sing. There is another option.

What if God himself is the melody you have been looking for and he is humming the tune in Jesus?

# What difference 2
# does it make?

## *Does personal faith have public implications?*

> I do not want my house to be walled in on all sides and my windows to be stifled. I want all the cultures of all lands to be blown about my house as freely as possible. But I refuse to be blown off my feet by any.[1]

> It is not the kings and generals that make history, but the masses of the people.[2]

So we begin to try to uncover the source of the melody of our lives. We try to sort out the jumble of notes and ideas in our heads that shape the way we view the world and our own place in it. It doesn't take long before we stumble across the role of faith. We have established that there is a role for faith in the world – we've even discovered that most people claim to have a faith of one kind or another – but what difference does that make?

It's one thing to recognize that faith[3] has a place in the public square, it's quite another to suggest that it has a place in our private lives! Yet who we are and what we think matters! 'What makes

---

1. Mohandas K. Gandhi.
2. Nelson Mandela.
3. From this point on, my arguments will flow from my own convictions as a Christian and follower of Christ.

you tick' is a very important question. All of us are influenced by something. We are products of millions of events, experiences and encounters. Sometimes the connection is very evident and sometimes it is hidden – but a connection is always there. Rosa Parks's experiences as a marginalized and excluded Black woman shaped her momentous decision not to give up her seat and move to the back of the bus in segregated Southern USA during the 1960s. Gandhi's commitments were shaped by his experiences both as a law student and as an Indian in the first half of the 20th century. He knew the importance of his own convictions in a world of diverse ideologies and conflicting beliefs. The truth is that from the way in which we have been parented, to the way in which we are educated, our views, ideas, preferences and perspectives are shaped by our lives and observations. To suggest otherwise is to fly in the face of sociology, psychology and common sense! As we read these words you will be making unconscious decisions about them. Are they true? Does what is being said here fit with our own perspective? Is it logical? Do we agree? What we think will shape the conclusions we come to.

Politicians, journalists and policy-makers have long recognized this principle. Some have even tried to fully enter the experience of another person for a period of time in order to try to understand how life works from a different point of view. There was at one time a trend for politicians to have stints of living rough, or surviving on benefits for a few weeks, to see what life might really be like 'on the other side'. Polly Toynbee, the British social commentator, journalist and one-time social affairs editor of the BBC, tried to live on the minimum wage on a council estate in 2003. She wrote about the challenges and struggles in her book *Hard Work*. In it she records the reaction of some of her friends and colleagues to what she was doing:

> But when I see people from my own world look so astonished at the idea that one of us could for a while live like one of them, I know how wide the gap still is.[4]

4. *Hard Work: Life in Low-pay Britain* by Polly Toynbee (London: Bloomsbury, 2003), chapter 2.

Of course, Toynbee is right – the gap is still very wide indeed. She is right precisely because our views and convictions are shaped by our experiences. Although her dip into living on a council estate and surviving on the minimum wage was temporary, her views were shaped by it. What we think and believe is determined by our *whole* life situation. I don't live in a vacuum, and nor do you. Our culture, our ethnicity and our communities shape us. Our social structures, our housing and our experience form our opinions. Our gender, our sexuality and our families shape our views and understandings. For the same reason, the faith that we hold has an important part to play in our lives and the way we view the world. In short, faith matters![5]

## Faith and breath

I've already argued that our values spring from a whole series of places and experiences in our lives – but one of those is undoubtedly the belief system that we have. Values cannot be contained in a private bubble. If values mean anything to us at all, then they shape how we live on the outside as well as the inside. If our values and our actions are not connected we end up in the worst form of hypocrisy. Our values are the oxygen of our actions. Ignoring our values is like cutting off the oxygen supply and it will suffocate our action. To suggest that our values must remain our own private opinions and be detached from our engagement in our society is a little like asking someone to breathe but not use their lungs. Such a separation is intellectually and physically impossible. What is true physically is also true spiritually. In order to *live* we must use our lungs and in order to engage coherently and consistently with the world, we *must* allow our values to shape our

5. Some might argue that faith doesn't matter because they don't have any faith. My arguments in Chapter 1 are worth looking at again, but the point I am trying to make is that even if you claim not to have any faith at all, that very statement shapes the way you view the world and how you engage in it. Such a deep-rooted conviction cannot be suspended when it comes to our engagement with our communities, our societies and our world.

actions. That doesn't mean that we always understand our values before we understand our actions, though. Sometimes we act without realizing why we act!

We don't work out how to breathe before we breathe! When I was a baby, I did not know I had lungs and I didn't 'learn' to breathe. I just did it. I breathed because that was what I did. As I grew up, though, I learned that I had two lungs and that without them I could not survive. In other words, I was *breathing* before I knew how or why I breathed. The same is true when it comes to the question of the connection between our actions, our values and our faith. Sometimes we do what we consider to be right long before we understand why we consider it to be right. We care for people instinctively, before we know *why* it is right to care for people. In the act of caring we show that we *value* people. But where did that *value* come from? Values come from all the influencers we have already discussed – and that includes faith. As a follower of Christ I now know that my valuing of people springs from the deep belief that every person is made in the image of God. And that *faith* conviction shapes my view of poverty, injustice, taxation and a whole range of other issues. So it is possible to behave in a certain way and hold a certain set of values and not always understand where they come from. However, if you do understand the 'lungs' of faith that lie behind the 'breath' of your values that in turn gives you the energy for your 'actions'. You are able to choose what you do and how you do it much more effectively.

One example of that is the development of a UK coalition called Churches for All. This coalition is a collection of organizations and groups that are motivated by Christian faith to serve and work alongside disabled people. The group sprung out of the experiences of the American, Joni Erikson-Tada, who was injured in a diving accident as a young woman. For over thirty years Joni, motivated by her Christian faith, has served and supported disabled people across the world. Churches for All came from the same Christian convictions. Christian faith shapes all that the coalition does in supporting people who are disabled and challenging both the Church and society to be more inclusive. To ask the coalition to carry out its work but to ignore their values is ridiculous. The very motivation to support and serve disabled people springs from Christian convictions around the image of God and human dignity which we will explore later.[6] Another example would be the work of drugs rehabilitation programmes in the UK and the US run by groups such as Teen Challenge. These groups see remarkable rates of recovery and re-entry to mainstream society by those who enter their rehabilitation centres. Yet the recovery programmes are designed with a Christian understanding of personhood, addiction and recovery at the centre. To ask Teen Challenge to suspend their Christian convictions but to continue to deliver their work is like asking them to live without breathing. The connection is as deeply rooted and as straightforward as that.[7]

On the other hand, there are some things that I previously did that I no longer do. My behaviour, values and actions have also been changed by understanding myself and my faith more. I am not the same person I was ten years ago – *because* my faith has strengthened some of my values and challenged others. That in turn has led to changed behaviour. My approach to the environment is one example. Ten years ago I was much less conscious of my responsibilities to the planet. However, my Christian faith has shaped the way I view the world and I now recognize much more clearly my responsibility to be more sustainable and responsible in the way I treat the environment. This is an example of my faith having shaped a value, which has subsequently changed my behaviour. My faith has shaped my values and they in turn have shaped my behaviour. That is a good thing. It is a good thing because my faith has given me a reliable plumb-line. Understanding *who* I am and what I *believe* means I am able to tie my actions and my convictions together and anchor them in a consistent view of the world and how to make it better.

Learning why I breathed and how to breathe has been helpful

---

6. For more information on Churches for All see www.churchesforall.org.uk.
7. Interestingly, this attempt to take the faith motivation out of service delivery is exactly what has happened in a number of cases in the UK. Teen Challenge in Wales have faced a real crisis of funding because they would not step away from the Christian nature of their programmes. Attempts to remove faith motivation from faith groups' activities is the equivalent of asking a political party to operate without its political ethos. It just won't work.

for me and for my family, however. One of my sons has a lung disorder.[8] It is still not fully diagnosed, but things are better now than they were when he was small. My wife, Debbie, and I spent a number of years knowing that there was something wrong with his lungs but not knowing how to treat the condition. So Benjamin would become very ill. He is now much better, but he still gets very ill. When he is well, we do not worry at all about how he breathes. However, when things go wrong, we really have to think about how his breathing works and rectify the problem. Understanding the physiology of his condition means we can treat it when things go wrong. It also means we can prevent the problems from occurring with medication and therapy.

The same is true for the role of faith in the public square. My aim is not to dismiss other religious perspectives; rather, it is to make the intellectual point that personal faith has a very important place in the public square. Our faith can help us to shape or to understand our own values. That in turn helps us to determine our own responses and actions. Sometimes those actions and values are instinctive; sometimes they are learned. In addition, understanding our views of society and how to address the challenges that society faces means that we have a set of convictions that will help us to treat the problems consistently. It will also mean that we are able to do some things that will stop some of the problems from happening in the first place. We cannot exclude faith from shaping our engagement in our societies. To do so is to remove at least one lung from individuals.

Arguing that faith has a place in public life is not the same thing as suggesting that faith should be *institutionalized* or *established*; I am not arguing for a re-invention of Christendom. Nor is it to suggest that faith should be publicly funded or that it should be prescriptive. I would not want to suggest for one moment that Britain or the US should give *only* Christian faith a place in the public square. It is *because* I am a follower of Christ that I believe that faith should have a place in the public square. I may not agree with what someone else might say, but I will defend their right to say it.

8. Benjamin's condition is similar to, but not the same as, cystic fibrosis.

## Diversity leads to a healthy society

Many of those reading this book are likely to come from either the USA or the UK. There is no doubt that both countries are very diverse societies. You only need to look at the cities of London and New York to see this. London is a mixed, cosmopolitan place, which claims to be the most diverse city in the world, with 37 different migrant communities of over 10,000 people. More than one in three of London's 7 million residents belong to an ethnic minority group, and the population encompasses 14 faiths and 300 languages.[9] London seeks to use all of that diversity and difference to its advantage. It takes the histories and backgrounds of its residents and celebrates 'the world in a city'. Diversity might have its challenges, but it can work.

New York has learnt the same lesson and applies the same principle. In fact, Michael Bloomberg acknowledged New York's diversity and strength in his state of the City address in 2006:

> Looking around at all of the elected officials and community leaders in this theater, I see faces with family roots in Africa, Asia, Europe, Latin America, the Caribbean. I see Jews, Christians, Muslims, Buddhists, gay and straight, immigrant and native-born. I see New York! The diversity of our City – and its leadership – gives us incredible strength. And over the past four years, as God knows, we have needed every ounce of it ...[10]

It is quite clear that diversity can lead to strength when diversity is understood and celebrated and differences are allowed to flourish alongside acceptance of responsibilities and obligations. When it is not understood, however, it leads to breakdown and there is division. Difference really does matter! It would be hard to find a logical argument against diversity. The American poet, Maya Angelou, is right:

9. Taken from website: http://www.nyu.edu/global/london/st_diversity.htm.
10. Taken from website: www.nyc.gov.

We all should know that diversity makes for a rich tapestry, and we must understand that all the threads of the tapestry are equal in value no matter what their color.[11]

Ninety per cent of Americans label themselves as religious in one way or another.[12] Yet in such a 'religious' nation, there are 200 million privately owned firearms compared to 140 million cars.[13] There are almost seven times as many airports as there are television stations.[14] Clearly the religious convictions of American citizens do not always impact the view they take of the environment or their attitude to preventing gun crime. Yet despite such startling statistics, there appears to be a growing desire within many Americans for a more just and ethical world. Growing numbers of Americans are searching for a connection between their spiritual convictions and the world in which they live.

Although Britain and the US are home to a plethora of religious convictions and spiritualities, there is some common ground that means we can find true strength in our diversity. There are some core values and principles that many spiritualities share. These common convictions are worth remembering as we try to work out ways in which those of different faiths and those of none can work together. Too often, we look for those things that divide us. Perhaps there is value in identifying common values and common commitments. If we can find it, we can build on the common good.

## The common good

African Traditionalists believe that people must have the courage to face life as it is and to endure both the sorrows and the joys, but that in order to build a better world individuals should be willing

---

11. Taken from the website:www.forbetterlife.org.
12. See *The Independent Guide to the US in Facts and Figures* published as an insert in the *Independent* Newspaper, 3 May 2006.
13. I find it staggering that there are more guns owned by US citizens than cars.
14. 14,893 airports compared to 2,218 television stations.

to sacrifice themselves for the sake of other people.[15] Those of the Bahai faith believe that the choice to prefer others over one's self is a conduit of blessing.[16] For Buddhists their founder's injunction not to hurt others with that which hurts them as individuals is a motivation for building a better world. Confusicianists believe that the person of perfect virtue must seek to establish others if they are to establish themselves. An individual must 'enlarge' others if they are to 'enlarge' themselves.[17] Hindus are convinced that duty and responsibility can be summed up in the principle that no one should do anything to another person if it would cause them pain to have the same thing done to themselves.[18] Jains believe that in happiness and suffering, in joy and in grief one person should regard other people as they do themselves.[19] Jews believe that they should not do to others what is hateful to themselves and that the whole of the Torah can be summed up in this. The rest, they believe, is just a commentary.[20] The prophet Mohammed said that an individual could not be a 'believer' until they wanted for other people what they wanted for themselves. Sikhism is committed to the principle that God is within us all, and therefore we should not do harm to others.[21] Zoroastrians believe that human nature is only good when it shall not do unto other people what it would consider bad for itself.[22]

As a follower of Christ, I can agree with all of these sentiments because they are reflected in the example and teaching of Christ that I should treat others as I would expect them to treat me.[23] As a citizen, I can recognize a shared value across faiths and work for a better world. I do not need to become a Sikh or a Muslim, etc. in order to see this uniting value and build upon it. My contention is simple – being a person of faith does not mean that you should privatize your faith in order to engage in the world. Nor does it

15. Kipsigis saying from Kenya.
16. Baha'u'llah, Tablet 71.
17. Analects 6.28.2.
18. Mahabharata, XIII: 114.
19. Mahavira.
20. Talmud, Shabbat 31a.
21. Guru Granth Sahib, p. 258.
22. Dadistan p I- Dinik, 94.5.
23. Matthew 7.12.

mean that you should force your faith on others before you will work with them. It means that you have a role in your community and society, because of your faith, not despite it.

## The challenge of faith

People of faith inherently want to treat others with respect. We are deeply committed to building healthy societies that allow for diversity, celebrate difference and encourage the discovery of common values. Yet society as a whole is not always good at acknowledging the importance of faith in building healthy communities. Privatized piety and fear of faith have led to chasms in understanding of how faith can shape a society. Faith is seen as a dangerous element in debates about society and its coherence. There are a number of reasons for this. It might be because we tend to caricature that which we do not understand – it's always easier to compare *our* best to *their* worst! It might also be because those who appear to be motivated by faith can appear to be extremists as well. As we have already seen, that can lead to us understanding 'faith' in terms of fundamentalism and negativity. However, it might just be because we have allowed ourselves to think that faith has nothing to do with pragmatics and real life. Somehow we have fallen into the trap of thinking that some things are 'sacred' or 'spiritual' and some things are not.

Religious people often strengthen that perception by the way in which they dichotomize their own lives. For example, many Christians in the UK and the US have sated their own consciences with attendance at a weekly church service on a Sunday morning. God seems to have become a commodity that fits in with their busy week. In a sense this dichotomy has meant that we have created a God who is very comfortable with us and with our preferences. He is boxed into 'Religious' activities and boxed out of relationships, finance, environmental responsibility and participation in our neighbourhoods. However, nothing could be further from the truth of what God intended our faith to be.

The Prime Minister, Tony Blair, delivered a speech for the

Faithworks Movement in March 2005 in which he said that faith should always be seen as private. Perhaps this attitude explains his reaction to a question put to him by British journalist Jeremy Paxman a few years earlier. Quizzing the Prime Minister over a meeting between Tony Blair and George W. Bush, Paxman asked the Prime Minister whether or not the President and Blair had prayed together. Tony Blair was dismissive of the question, replying, 'Of course we didn't pray together, Jeremy.' But what if faith is not privatized? To quote the American author, Jim Wallis, 'what if faith is personal, but never private?'[24] There is an alternative to suggesting that Blair, or Bush for that matter, should not let their 'private faith' get in the way of their public life. It might be healthy to accept that we are all shaped by our convictions, our beliefs and our spirituality. Having suggested that faith cannot be put in a box, how can any decision we make not be affected by it?

## Faith is an influencer

The faith that someone holds, whatever that faith might be, is a massive influence on that person's views. It cannot be anything else. The challenge of faith has arisen because we have allowed the idea of 'faith' to be misrepresented by moralists, fundamentalists and extremists. Not only that, we have allowed a very narrow definition of 'morality' to become the norm. We have allowed faith to be sidelined because we have allowed it to be hijacked. The United Kingdom and the United States have been shaped by Christian faith and values. From the right to freedom of expression to democracy itself, Christian faith has had a pivotal part to play. There are also people from other faith perspectives in our multicultural and diverse communities and they too have a right to allow their personal faith and convictions to shape their views of society. Our faith must not be consigned to the darkened rooms of

---

24. *God's Politics: Why the Right Gets it Wrong and the Left Doesn't Get it* by Jim Wallis (New York: HarperCollins, 2005).

a privatized and narrowly interpreted 'morality'. Instead, we must acknowledge two things.

First, the deep power of faith and the need to harness it for the good of our world and secondly, the breadth of morality and the fact that it touches on nearly all of our decisions. For those of us who hold a faith – however small it might be – we might then be able to understand how that faith can and does motivate us to build a better world. Christian motivation and morality is not reserved for those who feel passionately about abortion and marriage! Millions of people around the world, motivated by their Christian faith, fight injustice, engage with the causes of poverty and serve its victims, campaigning for a fairer, more equitable world. We must not allow ourselves to be marginalized. War, poverty and injustice are as much religious and moral issues as they are political ones. These are reasons that faith makes a difference.

> Religious faith brings a number of benefits – it provokes vision, integrity and a commitment to justice. It motivates individuals towards participating in this vision through personal responsibility and accountability. All the great religious traditions [ ... ] help to forge the neighbourly society in which people who would otherwise be on the margins are able to belong.[25]

## A living example

My argument in Chapter 1 was that faith is on the agenda for a lot of people. The fact that the 'idea' and 'role' of faith is on the agenda has further implications, though. The presence of faith in society is not something that can be denied, and its power to shape thinking and action is clear. That means that the personal motivation of faith – whether we have faith or not – moves from the edge of the agenda to the heart of the debate. People of faith are engaged in campaigning alongside those who have no faith and those who have a vague sense of spirituality. In 2005 millions of people in the UK took part in the Make Poverty History

25. Michael Howard, Faithworks Lecture, March 2005.

campaign. This was a campaign aimed at changing the minds of governments across the world on issues of poverty. It was a campaign for fair trade, debt cancellation and the eradication of poverty. Many of those who took part in the campaign were motivated by their faith in God and their view of other human beings as made in God's image. In the same way as the Jubilee Campaign of 2000 harnessed millions of people's support across the world for the cancellation of debt in Third World countries, Make Poverty History worked in 2005. Faith played an enormous role and had a massive impact that led to change. Faithworks is a Christian movement in the UK, which works with thousands of members and hundreds of partners. Every day communities across the length and breadth of Britain and the United States are served and changed by activists whose motivation is their faith. For them, and for those they help, faith matters!

## Faith is a change-bringer

Ask any one of those activists why they get out of bed every morning and they will tell you it is because of their faith. This is not something they are trying to force on other people, but it is not an irrelevance either! They are committed to seeing the good in others, to respecting people who are different, to working shoulder to shoulder with other Christians, those of other faiths and those of none in order to build a healthier community and a better world. Faith is alive and well and bringing change in millions of lives across the world.

A Christian faith that is not aligned with the great issues of justice, the dignity of humanity and overcoming poverty deserves to be sidelined and marginalized because it is not an authentic demonstration of faith. However, for true change to take place, faith must always be present. That is because genuine transformation never starts from the outside and works in. Social transformation cannot take place without inner spiritual transformation. This is not to suggest a narrow conversionist approach to life. Instead it is to acknowledge that true change must be holistic.

Changing a person's circumstances does not always change a person's view of themselves. The latter cannot be done 'to' anyone. It is a change that must happen from within – and must spring from faith. The recent increase in self-identification of people with faith, particularly Christian faith, as highlighted in Chapter 1, is striking. The comments of pop stars and politicians and heads of state make it pretty clear that the connection between personal faith and public service is being rediscovered on both sides of the Atlantic.

## An interesting test

Having outlined the challenge and motivation of Christian faith and acknowledged that faith has changed millions of lives across the world and through the centuries, let me suggest an interesting test. In order to gauge the impact of Christian faith on the UK or the US, ask what these nations might look like if Christian faith was not present.

The reality is that Christians and their engagement in the challenges of their communities and their societies down through the years have brought about massive societal change for the better. From the abolition of slavery to penal, educational and housing reform, Christians have been trailblazers in change. Whether they choose to accept it or not, the British Labour party was birthed in Methodism and has a deep link to Christian motivation. In the UK, the welfare state, nursing care, the hospice movement and civil liberties have all been enhanced and protected by Christian faith. The Civil Rights Movement in the USA, the development of the US constitution and the very form of democracy and liberty that is so often celebrated by American citizens all have their roots in Christian faith.

What would happen to the most marginalized, the most excluded and the poorest in our communities if the people working with them motivated by their own faith withdrew? Government funding could not sustain the programmes being delivered on either side of the Atlantic Ocean. A removal of the tireless service and unstinting devotion of millions of people of faith would result in a collapse of the infrastructure of both the United States and the United Kingdom. In short, our communities would collapse. There is a deeper challenge that we could consider, however, to help us work out whether faith matters. While it is easy to think about a national picture, or a general trend, it is much more challenging to think about something personally. What would the removal of faith mean in my community? What would it mean for my life? What would it mean for my street? These deeply penetrating questions begin to unearth for us the depth of connection between faith and life.

The contribution and vitality of faith-motivated action is clear. Without it the communities of which we are each a part would disintegrate. Faith has proven its worth. Those of us who are motivated to build a better world face the challenge of allowing our own faith once again to be something we are neither afraid of nor embarrassed by.

## What difference does it make?

So in answering the question that we set out to explore at the beginning of this chapter, there is a deep challenge for us. Both those who are motivated by faith and those who are helped and served by such people know that faith makes a difference – either directly or indirectly. More broadly, a society that cannot celebrate faith is an impoverished society. For every one of us, faith is as much an issue of diversity as gender or ethnicity. To pretend it is not is to be intolerant and dismissive of the deepest motivator for good in millions of peoples' lives. Hillary Clinton was right in her analysis:

> What we have to do ... is to find a way to celebrate our diversity and debate our differences without fracturing our communities.[26]

26. Taken from the website: www.forbetterlife.org.

# What difference does it make?

The Irish author, Jonathan Swift,[27] famous for his book, *Gulliver's Travels*, once said that we had just enough religion to make us hate, but not enough to make us love one another. That is probably also true of modern British and American life. Politicians and opinion formers are in danger of caricaturing the presence and contribution of Christians and other faiths at their peril. A lack of understanding and lack of engagement with faith communities impoverishes everyone.

That is not to suggest that we must tolerate religiously motivated hatred, intolerance or discrimination – far from it. Striving for fairness, equality and inclusion are surely the benchmarks of a healthy society and a balanced life. Just think what the world would be like if everyone in it was like you or me! As we move on, though, it is important to note that the questions we have been addressing in this chapter are not detached from our own lives. Answering the question 'does it matter?' in a non-personal way is somehow letting ourselves off the hook. Our community and our society is not made up of an amorphous presence, it is made up of people like you and me. If faith matters at all, then it must matter to me and to you. That is not to suggest that you must become like me, but it does imply that you and I have a responsibility to understand ourselves, our world and one another. Britain and the United States are not 'melting pots' of ideas and cultures, they are mosaics. A mosaic allows for every piece to have its place – a melting pot tries to make them all combine to make something that is indistinguishable. The values I hold, the contribution I make and the part I play in building a better world are decisions that I must make for myself.

In the first centuries of the Church, a great debate erupted over the relevance of Christian faith to philosophy and ideology. Athens, the centre of thinking, civic debate and 'progressive thought' sat in apparent juxtaposition to Jerusalem, the geographic motherland of the early church family. The early church Father, Tertullian, articulated the debate in this simple phrase:

---

27. Jonathan Swift (1667–1745).

What has Athens to do with Jerusalem? [28]

For almost four hundred years the Church debated what it meant to hold a set of values shaped by Christian faith and take your place in society. Could and should Christians join the army? Should they worship Caesar? Should they deny their faith for the good of their homelands? How should they treat the poor?

At the beginning of the fourth century the Roman emperor Constantine apparently became a follower of Christ and the era of Christendom was born. This was an era when the Christian Church became a power holder and power broker. It was never what the Church was called to be. It led to abuses of power that any follower of Christ is ashamed of. The Church became an enforcer. It mistakenly and brutally tried to *force* people to believe. That approach never worked. The relationship between faith and public life was debated throughout that period. Can you have such a thing as a Christian nation? What would such a nation look like? What do you do with those who do not share your faith, but share your concerns for the world?[29]

In the post-war era, the relationship between Christian faith and the state has again been under the microscope. The collapse of the power relationship between the Church and the state is something that many of us as followers of Christ welcome. This collapsing empire and structure means that we can now investigate the questions that have been asked for two thousand years from a much more pragmatic and personal level. The arguments around faith and society have raged throughout the history of the Church, and will continue to rage. The argument is now taking place in a different place, though.

The relationship between faith and society matters because it moves away from the compartmentalization of lives and communities and begins to address the problems of our society holistically. Christian faith recognizes the deep connections across the whole of life. How we treat people as equals and as those who

---

28. Tertullian, *De Praescriptione Haereticorum* 7.9.
29. For a fantastic critique of Christendom see *Post-Christendom: Church and Mission in a Strange New World* by Stuart Murray-Williams (Milton Keynes: Authentic, 2004).

share our world, our aspirations and our obligations really does matter. The challenges to be overcome are too great for sociologists, politicians, academics or humanitarians. They are too great for theologians or philosophers or idealists. Building a better world must be a team effort and to succeed it must treat people as whole people – not only in addressing their needs, but also in tapping into their motivation and their inspiration. Faith is a strong motivator to action, but also to aspiration. We cannot ignore it or sideline it; to do so would be to disengage millions of activists or to tell them their motivation must be separated from their action.

Yet there is still a need for a better understanding of what Christian faith contributes to our communities and to the world. It is not enough to read the words of pop stars and politicians – we need to know *how* Christian faith helps build a better world. We need to understand some of the positive principles that underpin Christian faith if we are to understand what it can contribute to our lives and to the world. As the leader of a Christian social movement, I am convinced that followers of Christ have a great deal to contribute to making the world a better place, but I also believe that it is vital that we understand the contribution of others. Christian faith must understand its own unique contribution to building a better world,[30] but it must also understand how others can contribute to making the world a better place.

We must somehow 'get under the skin' of Christian faith to explore the principles that flow from it. What exactly are the principles and commitments that flow from Christian faith that can help to make the world a better place? This becomes a fundamental question because the answer to the question sets the compass that guides the way we act. If those who hold a Christian worldview do not understand what motivates us, we will become suspicious of others too easily. For fear of losing our own distinctive identity, we will withdraw from partnerships and collaborations. Such withdrawal often demonstrates our apprehensions and uncertainties about ourselves. Isolation may be wrapped in words of 'purity' and 'preservation of identity' but more often than not it happens

---

30. I have included an Appendix that outlines what I believe to be core principles for a Christian Social Movement.

because of a lack of self-understanding and confidence. Understanding the principles and commitments that guide my own life make me more ready and able to explore partnerships with others confidently. If I can understand how my faith can change the world, then I can work with others who want to make the world a better place. I need to understand my own compass if I am to navigate my relationships with others well.

# Part II

## Christian Principles?

# A charter for change

3

*What are the guiding principles of building a better world from the Christian faith?*

> There is a Christianity ... which takes off fetters instead of binding them on – that breaks every yoke – that lifts up the bowed down.[1]

Compasses only ever point in one direction – north! If you don't set the compass properly you can end up way off track. As we begin to explore the 'compass' of Christian faith in this chapter, it's worth noting that there is a bit of readjustment in our thinking that is needed. Christian faith has become more known for what it opposes than what it supports! Such a reputation is a serious misalignment of the compass, and it needs to be corrected before we can proceed. You cannot build a better world simply by criticizing the one that exists.

It is important to protest at those things that seem to be so wrong with the world. Protests only lead to change, however, when we have a view of how things should be, not just how things should not be. As I pointed out earlier, there is an unspoken understanding that it is much easier to be in opposition than it is to be in government. That is because when in opposition it is easy to

---

1. Frederick Douglass, former slave and prominent US abolitionist.

criticize, to malign and to point out faults. However, when in government, the responsibility is to make things work. Governing means the privilege of being able to complain and to attack is replaced by the obligation to *do* something. Protest has been replaced with responsibility. The most effective argument for change is a new vision of what the future could be. We will only change the world if we have an idea of what it needs to become, and how it can change. As Jim Wallis says, protest might be good, but alternatives are better.[2]

All of the spirituality of Christian faith springs from belief in a God who *is* love and wants the best for the world he has created and the people he has made. So even his injunctions and guidance on what we should not do are motivated by a deep desire for the best for us. It is because he knows us and has a positive view of us that he has given us things like commandments and warnings. When we take these injunctions out of context we create a caricature of Christian faith, and caricatures aren't normally that flattering – or honest! This caricature of Christian faith can even make God a bad-tempered old man who looks forward to reprimanding his pupils and showing them how worthless they are. This is not only a caricature of God; it is a gross distortion of who he is and what he is like.

If the hypothesis I am suggesting is true, and Christian faith provides a foundation for a spirituality that can truly build a better world, then it is vitally important to work out what things this faith believes *in*, not just understand what it stands against. I want to do two things in the next two chapters. First, in this chapter, I want to explore a specific charter for change. Secondly, in the next chapter, I want to unpack a Christian response to some key areas of life in modern society.

---

2. Jim Wallis, *God's Politics*, chapter 4.

## Discovering a charter for change

A Christian charter for change does exist. It is not just a sound-bite manifesto or an easy-to-follow instruction guide. Instead it is a charter that has the power to transform us, our communities and our world. It is widely known as the Sermon on the Mount.

The Sermon on the Mount is the most challenging charter for change in history. It was delivered by Jesus on a hillside in Palestine. Like a hammer breaking shackles, Jesus' words brought hope and freedom to those who listened. He painted a picture of spiritual and social transformation that was utterly different to institutionalized Religion and spiritual practice. Gandhi, who never embraced Christian faith but admired Christ, was inspired by it and troubled by the fact that the Church in the West treated it so lightly:

> The message of Jesus as I understand it is contained in the Sermon on the Mount unadulterated and taken as a whole ... If then I had to face only the Sermon on the Mount and my own interpretation of it, I should not hesitate to say, 'Oh, yes, I am a Christian.' But negatively I can tell you that in my humble opinion, what passes as Christianity is a negation of the Sermon on the Mount ... I am speaking of the Christian belief, of Christianity as it is understood in the west.[3]

The Sermon on the Mount remembers the forgotten, lifts the downtrodden, gives hope to the despairing and worth to those who have been devalued. It is in this moving discourse that we find a number of principles that can guide our actions, our attitudes and our intentions. The full message is contained in Matthew's Gospel in the New Testament from the beginning of chapter five through to the end of chapter seven. You might want to stop reading this book and read that small section of the New Testament before we proceed.

3. As quoted in an article entitled 'Gandhi vs. Christ' to be found at http://www.geocities. com/orthopapism/gandhi.html. For more information on Gandhi and his comments on Christian faith and the influence of Christ upon his life, see *Gandhi on Christianity* edited by Robert Ellsberg (Maryknoll, NY: Orbis Books, 1991).

The beginning of the Sermon on the Mount has become known as the Beatitudes, because it promises 'blessing' or 'fulfilment' or 'contentment' to those who adhere to it.[4] In just a few dazzling statements, Jesus set out a way of life that has the power to transform the world.

Now when he saw the crowds, he went up to a mountainside and sat down. His disciples came to him, and he began to teach them, saying:

Blessed are the poor in spirit, for theirs is the Kingdom of Heaven.
Blessed are those who mourn, for they shall be comforted.
Blessed are the meek, for they will inherit the earth.
Blessed are those who hunger and thirst after righteousness for they will be filled.
Blessed are the merciful for they shall be shown mercy.
Blessed are the poor in heart, for they shall see God.
Blessed are the peacemakers, for they will be called the Sons of God.
Blessed are those who are persecuted because of righteousness, for theirs is the Kingdom of Heaven.[5]

Within these words lie key principles that can transform both our own lives and the lives of those around us:

1. Poor people matter and God is on their side.[6]
2. Grief and pain may be a part of life, but there is hope.[7]
3. Power will be given to those who should have it.[8]
4. Striving for justice in the world is a good thing to do and it will eventually work.[9]

---

4. The word 'beatitude' has its roots in a sense of purpose, contentment and 'blessing', literally meaning 'you will be happy'.
5. Matthew 5.1–10.
6. Blessed are the poor in spirit, for theirs is the Kingdom of Heaven.
7. Blessed are those who mourn, for they shall be comforted.
8. Blessed are the meek, for they will inherit the earth.
9. Blessed are those who hunger and thirst after righteousness for they will be filled.

5. Compassionate action evokes compassionate response.[10]
6. All of us have faults, but we can all reach our God-given potential.[11]
7. Peacemaking is vital and reflects God's heart.[12]
8. Opposition to such a lifestyle is guaranteed, but it will not defeat this lifestyle.[13]

My aim in addressing each of these principles is not to unpack them fully, but instead to explore very briefly the extent to which they connect with life. Unpacking each fully in the context of modern living would mean a much lengthier book than you have in your hand. The principles build on one another and act like a staircase for a fairer and better world.

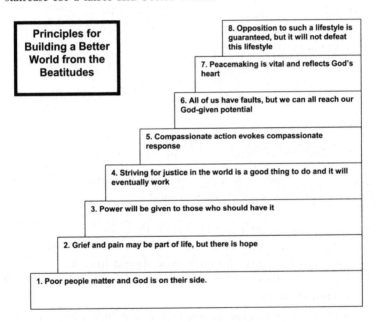

10. Blessed are the merciful for they shall be shown mercy.
11. Blessed are the poor in heart, for they shall see God.
12. Blessed are the peacemakers, for they will be called the Sons of God.
13. Blessed are those who are persecuted because of righteousness, for theirs is the Kingdom of Heaven.

## Principle 1: Poor people matter and God is on their side

*Blessed are the poor in spirit, for theirs is the Kingdom of Heaven.*

It is impossible to read the New Testament accounts of the life of Jesus without being challenged by how much he engages with the poor. He fed the poor when they were hungry. He spent time with those that his society had written off as useless or worthless. He went against social and religious trends of the day to embrace and care for the sick, the outcast and the lonely.

In fact the whole of the Bible makes it clear that poor people matter deeply to God. Physical poverty or wealth are some of the central themes of the Bible. Money and possessions and how we use them are probably the most present issues in the Older Testament.[14] The New Testament contains in excess of 500 direct references to wealth and material possessions (that is a mention in one of every 16 verses). In the books of Matthew, Mark and Luke, one verse in every ten is about poverty and wealth. In Luke the ratio drops to one verse in every seven. In James it is one in every five. Jesus talked about money and wealth more than he did about heaven, hell, sexual practice, obeying the Torah or the issue of violence.[15] As we will see later, when Jesus spoke in the synagogue in Nazareth outlining why he had come, the first thing he said was that he had come to preach good news to the poor.[16]

The important thing to note about the attitude of God to the poor is this – he is on their side. What we do not see Jesus doing is *just* talking about the poor. He serves them. He feeds them, listens to them, defends them and understands them. That is also

14. The 'Old Testament' is the name given by Christians to the Hebrew Bible. I am using the name 'Older Testament' because I think 'Old' could be interpreted as irrelevant. The Christian New Testament cannot be understood without reference to the Older Testament because so much of Christian faith is rooted in Jewish understanding and faith. It's also very important to remember that both the Older and the Newer Testaments are understood by followers of Christ as special writings that inform our thinking, our lives and our relationships with God and each other.

15. See *The Call to Conversion* by Jim Wallis (Abingdon: Marston Books, 2006), p. 57.

16. See Luke 4.16–17.

because he himself was poor. As far as we know he never had wealth and he never even owned a house. He also cared about the structures and the systems that made people poor, and kept them poor.

Christian spirituality does not mean that God just understands the poor from a neutral point of view. He stands on their side. He has *become* one of them. We cannot claim to be authentically Christian if we have not committed to serving the poor and to helping them. In following Jesus, we follow the one who leads us to the poor. There are many kinds of poverty, and Christian faith calls us to confront it wherever it is found. Jim Wallis suggests that there are three faces to poverty.[17] *Material* poverty is the most obvious form of poverty, but he argues that many live with *civic* poverty – exclusion from decision-making and the denial of the opportunity to shape their own future. Their voices are not heard or are used by those with power as pawns for change.[18] He also rightly identifies that *spiritual* poverty exists and that this affects all people. This is the yearning and longing for discovery of our true purpose. It is looking for a connection to God that can deal with the mistakes of our past, the challenges of our present and give us hope and strength for the future. I would add two other 'faces' of poverty. The first is a poverty of *identity*. This is where people are told that they do not matter, that they are worth less than others or that they are useless. This is a poverty connected with a person's past and their history. The second 'face' of poverty I would add is one of *aspiration*. This occurs when people are told that they cannot change, that their destiny and their tomorrows are determined by the mistakes or the experiences of the past only. This is a poverty connected with a person's future.

For me, five faces of poverty are important – material, civic, spiritual poverties and poverties of identity and aspiration. All of them are directly spoken to in the first beatitude because Jesus promises those of us who live with such poverty that *the Kingdom of Heaven* is ours.

17. *Faithworks* by Jim Wallis (London: SPCK, 2000), chapter 5, pp. 51ff.
18. We need to be careful that when we work with the poor we do not look down on them. This is a real danger for those who think they are 'better' than the poor. I'll unpack this in a moment.

This promise has an incredibly deep meaning. The phrase *the Kingdom of Heaven* was adopted by devout Jews because they did not want to use the actual name of God himself. The reason for that was that they did not want to break the commandment given to them by Moses,[19] which forbade the unnecessary use of God's name. So when Jews used the phrase *Kingdom of Heaven* they were referring to their relationship with God himself – his character, his commitments and his priorities. In other words Jesus said that those who are poor *in any way* have the promise that God himself is on their side. He is with them. In fact, in Jesus, he is one of them. And what kind of God is it that is with us? A look at the name of God can help us see the kind of God who is 'with' the poor. His name is found throughout the Bible. Obviously Jesus is the clearest example of his name. Jesus means 'God rescues'. He is also called Emmanuel which means 'God is with us'. He is also called the 'Messiah' or 'Christ' which both have the same meaning: 'anointed one' or 'special messenger'. When Moses wanted to know what God was like, he asked him, and God showed his nature to Moses. He revealed himself as:

> The Lord, the Lord, the compassionate and gracious God, slow to anger, abounding in love and faithfulness, maintaining love to thousands and forgiving wickedness, rebellion and sin.[20]

Those who express Christian faith and seek to develop a Christian spirituality and approach to life cannot do so and at the same time ignore the poor.

> These goals – clean water for all; school for every child; medicine for the afflicted; an end to extreme and senseless poverty – these are not just any goals; they are the Millennium Develop-

---

19. These are often summarized as the 'Ten Commandments'; they can be found in the Older Testament at the beginning of chapter 20 in the second book of the Bible, Exodus.
20. For the fuller story and context of this, read Exodus chapters 33 and 34. This description of God is found Exodus 34.6.

ment goals ... And they are more than that. They are the
Beatitudes for a globalised world.[21]

# Principle 2: Grief and pain may be a part of life, but there is hope

*Blessed are those who mourn for they shall be comforted.*

Grief and despair are threads of modern life that know no barrier.
They are woven into our lives from an early age and are part of
what it means to be truly human. As surely as we all enjoy laughter,
at some point in our lives we will also endure tears. While there is
no doubt that those who are poor feel pain and grief, all of us suffer
loss. From the loss of someone we love, to the failure of a dream,
the collapse of a plan or the impact of financial distress, we mourn.
There is no way to avoid it. Yet at the heart of the charter that we
are exploring is the promise by Jesus that those who mourn shall be
comforted.

Mourning and grief may be part of our experience as human
beings, but how we handle it differs widely. For some, the pain
and the distress of loss or the impact of sudden change can be
impossible to recover from. Those with faith and those without it
face the same dangers, the same fears and the same losses. Yet Jesus
makes a specific promise to those who mourn or grieve – they will
be comforted. In its narrowest sense this promise means that the
tears and the pain that we feel will pass. It is not as much a promise
that we will never go through grief, as it is a promise that we will
go *through* it and don't have to stay locked in it.

For the person caught in the pain of grief, it can feel like there is
no way out, but Jesus tells us that there is. There are hundreds of
references to grief and pain and to comfort in the Bible – more
than I could recount to you here. But the summary of all of the

21. Keynote address given by Bono at the National Prayer Breakfast, 2 February 2006, Washington DC.

promises is found here in this simple beatitude or blessing – the pain will not last forever. This is not always easy to believe; yet hearing the promise from another can help. Knowing that a way through exists, even when you do not know precisely what that way is, can make a difference. You may not know how to get through difficult times, but Christian faith leads to a connection with God that helps you remember that even if you don't know how to get through what you face, you know that there is a God who understands and who can and will help.

In its broader sense this principle points away from despair and to hope. It is so easy to see the society in which we live as unchangeable. We can convince ourselves that things *cannot* change. This can lead us to deep disillusionment and to deep despair, which in turn leads to grief. For those of us committed to building a better world, we can feel like the mountain is too large to climb. You can feel like you make a difference in one situation only to be confronted with another. What keeps you going when your own energy saps and your own strength is gone? At the beginning of the 20th century there was a genuine sense of hope and optimism that humanity could now take care of itself, and that somehow we would get out of the mess that we were in. That we would learn to love one another more, that we would eradicate war and that we could actually defeat disease, pain and banish want. At the beginning of the 21st century we now realize that pain and life go together, and that no matter how hard we try we will never change the world on our own. There is a stronger realization in 2006 that we need help and something beyond ourselves to change our world than there was in 1906. The principle of this second beatitude tells us that because God is there, there is hope.

This principle of hope as opposed to cynicism or defeatism is not the same as self-motivation. I am not suggesting that we should dig deeper for another bit of motivation. Quite the opposite! This principle helps me understand that it is only when I recognize that I *cannot* do it on my own that I realize that there is someone who can help. I break my heart because of my own pain or the pain in the world. I mourn because it seems impossible to change the world – and yet it is at that moment I am given the courage and the confidence and the strength to keep going because I remember again that this fight is not just my fight. This cause is not just my cause. God is on my side.

I would be amazed if anyone reading these words has not at some point felt like things were hopeless, particularly those of us who strive for justice, who long for freedom, who detest poverty and loathe exclusion. Each of us lies awake at night and wonders what to do to make it better, to change the way things are. This principle is for those moments. It is a reminder that things will not always be this way – God will comfort those who mourn. He will change the world. But he will do it through the hands, feet and hearts of people like you and me.

Christian spirituality points beyond ourselves to God, but it does not sacrifice our identities to do it. Instead, we are pointed to God, who then points back to us and takes us on a journey with him. My spirituality tells me that I do not labour on my own. There is no situation of poverty, exclusion, loss or pain either personal or communal that God has not reached before me. There is no situation that is beyond change. There is no one and nothing beyond hope.

That keeps me going.

## Principle 3: Power will be given to those who should have it

*Blessed are the meek, for they will inherit the earth.*

Meekness is a word that is often misunderstood. It can be misinterpreted as weakness, or the inability to do something, when it actually means the ability to hold your strength in tension with your patience. The third principle behind the Sermon on the Mount reminds us of that. The promise is that those who must restrain their strength will one day be entrusted with the power that is theirs. Just imagine the impact of these words on the initial audience. Surrounded by Roman oppressors and held down by strict and legalistic religious leaders, Jesus reminds his listeners that their 'submission' and meekness is not futile. They will win through in the end. Restraining their strength is the right thing to do. Perhaps Jesus picked up this theme later in the Sermon on the Mount when he taught the principles of non-violence and non-aggression? He certainly lived out this principle in enduring the humiliation of rejection by his own people, beating by Roman soldiers and ultimately crucifixion and death.

For the Jews of first-century Palestine this would have been as hard a pill to swallow as it is for us today. It was a hard pill to swallow for Gandhi – but he was committed to non-aggression and the conviction that power would be given to those who should have it, and his approach worked. It is also the principle that guided Martin Luther King Jr. The Civil Rights Movement was founded on the principle of non-retaliation. King recognized that striving to *take* power would never work. Progress could not be forcibly created, but it could be sacrificially ushered in. The greatest strength would be to endure, to be convinced that change would come:

> Human progress is neither automatic nor inevitable ... Every step toward the goal of justice requires sacrifice, suffering, and struggle; the tireless exertions and passionate concern of dedicated individuals.[22]

The principle that was true for first-century Palestine, for an emerging independent India and for the Civil Rights protesters of the USA is also true today. The example of Jesus and his teaching point away from force, aggression and violence and toward endurance and continued perseverance. Such endurance and continued perseverance are made possible with the solid promise that power *will* be redistributed. The moral force of the previous two beatitudes give greater strength to this principle, though – the poor have God on their side and a recognition of our own powerlessness connects us to the greatest strength possible. The longing for a better world will be answered.

22. See http://www.brainyquote.com/quotes/quotes/m/martinluth164280.html for more details of this quotation from Martin Luther King, Jr.

Furthermore, this spirituality of ultimate hope and success gives a greater ability to endure the present pain and conflict. Following Jesus creates a greater vista, a further horizon and a higher purpose for the follower; it reminds us of the connectedness of life and the ultimate rebalance of power to those who have been denied it for so very long.

## Principle 4: Striving for justice in the world is a good thing to do and it will eventually work

*Blessed are those who hunger and thirst after righteousness for they will be filled.*

The words for righteousness and justice are very close to one another in Greek, which is the language in which the New Testament was written.[23] This closeness is shown in what Jesus said as recorded here. The longing for a better, fairer world is deeply rooted. The promise of God, through Christ, is that it will result in the fulfilment of the longing itself.

Earlier in the chapter the diagram that I used for the eight principles was a set of steps. This is because the beatitudes can be seen to lead on from one to another. The connectedness of the statements becomes clearer as we progress through them. The reality of poverty challenges us to do something; it causes a reaction in our hearts and our passions are raised, because we *know* that something must be done. God reminds us that the poor have his heart. This leads to a great despair at the world in which we live. Why is their poverty not overcome now? Our own pain and the pain of others is something that we somehow experience. It is

23. The actual word for both righteousness and justice is linked to the Hebrew word 'Tsidkenu', transliterated '*tsedeq*', and the Greek word '$\delta\iota\kappa\alpha\iota o\sigma\grave{u}\nu\eta$', transliterated '*dikaiosune*'. For those who want to explore this further, take a look at the following reference: *The Analytical Lexicon to the Greek New Testament* by William D. Mounce (Michigan: Zondervan, 1993), p. 148 and *New International Dictionary of Old Testament Theology* edited by Willem A. VanGemeren (Carlisle: Paternoster Press, 1997), vol. I, p. 813ff and column 3, p. 764f.

something that we *know* is true even if we do not know how we know it. Almost like an intuition, we mourn the pain in our lives and in the world. The pain of poverty and injustice is almost unbearable. God reminds us that ultimately comfort will replace this mourning. This grief propels us forward, but it will not last forever. The mourning that springs from injustice itself leads to a deep sense that power must be shifted – that those whose voices are not heard should be heard. It is perhaps at this point that many of us want to *force* change. Because of the depth of our feeling, we are tempted to take power ourselves and try to *make change happen*. God reminds us that we cannot do that and that instead he promises that the change process we are part of will see success. This then leads us to the fourth principle of building a better world – that we must continue in the struggle because it will eventually work.

We must remember this truth in our darkest moments. I am convinced that this *longing* or *ache* for justice is one of the most uniting passions of humanity. Whether we are Christians, Jews, Muslims, Sikhs, Buddhists, or of no faith, we are tied together by this *hunger* and this *thirst* for a better world, and for justice. And this hunger and thirst directly flows from our shared humanity and the truth that we each bear the image of God in some way. The depth of this longing to do something that will make a difference cannot and should not be underestimated, though. Consider this prayer of St Francis of Assisi:

> Where there is discord, may we bring harmony.
> Where there is error, may we bring truth.
> Where there is doubt, may we bring faith.
> Where there is despair, may we bring hope.

We may consider those things that we do to be small things. Giving to charity, buying fair-trade produce, volunteering to help in a project, sending a postcard as part of a lobbying campaign or writing to an elected representative to ask for a change of policy on debt. These things in and of themselves may seem to be insignificant, but they are not. They are the ways in which our longing for justice, and desire to see a better world work themselves out in our lives. But what if they are all motivated by a desire for the *common good*? What if God is in each one? Then we become part of a movement that can change the world. We are no longer just unrelated individuals doing little things; instead we are each part of a much *bigger* thing.

The promise of Christian faith, a promise that we hold on to, is that justice will come. Inequality will be overcome. The very longing that we feel for such change is promise of the change itself. God has placed this in all people and the fact that the longing exists is met by the promise that it will be satisfied. Like a child crying for milk from her mother's breast, God hears the cry of people for justice on the earth, and just as a mother will not deny her child food, God will not deny justice to the people of the world.

## Principle 5: Compassionate action evokes compassionate response

*Blessed are the merciful for they shall be shown mercy.*

Here we have the principle of reciprocity. Our merciful action to other people will evoke merciful response to us in them. If we are to see the world become a better place, we must treat people mercifully. Once again, the impact of these words on the original hearers would have been profound. The first reaction of oppressed people is not always to show mercy. Instead it is to react, to lash out. The last principle we examined was that justice will be done. A natural consequence of believing that could be to become the arbitrators of that justice ourselves. The fifth principle provides clear parameters by which to understand the fourth. We are not the ultimate source of justice – God is. Jesus was telling his listeners that if they chose to hit out at their oppressors they would evoke a similar response. However, if they showed compassion and mercy to other people, that compassion would eventually be reciprocated.

Remember that these principles are set within the context of Jesus making promises to his hearers. He was saying this – *as you show mercy to others, you will be shown mercy.* He did *not* say that mercy would flow back from the recipient. That might be the case, but it is not always. However, there is a deeper principle here.

The BBC, in the early spring of 2006, screened a series of programmes in which they gave victims of violence in Northern Ireland the chance to meet, at times to confront, the perpetrators of that violence. These meetings were loosely based on the South African Truth and Reconciliation Commission, and like the Commission, they involved the Archbishop Desmond Tutu. The meetings were harrowing. The pain and loss in both the victims and the perpetrators were clearly demonstrated. Perhaps I found them more deeply moving because I am from Northern Ireland, I'm not sure. What I do know is that as I watched and listened I did not always see mutual forgiveness and reconciliation. Mercy offered was sometimes returned, but not always. However, I could not help but feel that a whole community was being changed by these encounters, not only those sat at the table. As I watched I was forced to put myself in the place of those that sat there and to think about how *I* would react, what *I* would say or do. And I know that hundreds of thousands of other Irish people did the same. Somehow the healing that needs to take place in Northern Ireland is *both* personal and communal. Yet the principle of this beatitude is that communal mercy and personal mercy are deeply connected. If we want to live in a tolerant and merciful society, we *have* to display tolerance, compassion and mercy. That mercy might not always be reciprocated but it will change something beyond just that one encounter.

The Christian principle is simple, yet profound. We cannot create a fair and caring world by engaging in activities or harbouring attitudes that militate against fairness and compassion. To do so is to continue the cycle. The moment we choose to be merciful, however, we break a link in the chain and thus weaken the chain itself. In other words, we break the chain, a link at a time.

## Principle 6: All of us have faults, but we can all reach our God-given potential

*Blessed are the pure in heart, for they shall see God.*

The steps of these principles continue. In order to show mercy to other people, we need to somehow realize the depth of our own need for mercy. This is honest appraisal of our own faults and shortcomings. It is a purity of heart that enables us to recognize our need for mercy from others as much as other people's need for mercy from us. Mercy can never truly be shown when we feel we are also using power. Had I been listening to Jesus on the hillside in Palestine, I would have wanted to know how I could possibly show mercy to those who had hurt me. But I think that even before I could have asked the question he would have provided me with the answer in this beatitude. I just need to stop and think about my own prejudices and faults honestly for a moment and it will enable me to realize how much mercy I need – and therefore I become free to show mercy.

The promise of Jesus is that the pure in heart will see God. That means that when we are honest about ourselves we are able to encounter God and thus become all that we *can* be rather than what we are. The passion for justice and a better world cannot possibly be contained in the conviction that we can feed people, and build houses for them and thus overcome injustice. Material, spiritual and civic poverty as well as poverty of identity and aspiration must be overcome for the world to be a fairer place. From the areas of the United Kingdom where deprivation is rife to the ghettos of urban America, poverty will only be overcome when there is a realization of our own involvement in injustice and our need for change personally. Other people are as entitled to reach their God-given potential as I am. They are as marred by mistakes and bad judgements as I am. Both they and I must look beyond our existing selves to discover our potential. The most obvious place to look is to the source of our lives. For the Christian, this is God. When we are honest about ourselves we are able to become the people that we were born to be. Until we are honest in our hearts, 'pure' as Jesus said, we are not able to move forward to what we can become.

## Principle 7: Peacemaking is vital and reflects God's heart

*Blessed are the peacemakers for they will be called the Sons of God.*

So we reach the next step. When we realize that we are as much in need of change and transformation as those whom we live alongside – both those we love and those we do not – we become aware of the importance of living *together*. First-century Palestine was a hotbed of zealots and terrorists – people who were going to *take* power and *force* change. Yet Jesus tells them that those who are peacemakers are those who reflect God's heart. His implication is clear: when we act to bring peace, unity and harmony we act most like God. In other words, when we are motivated by love rather than hate or anger, we most display the character of God. This is as challenging now as it was then.

As I write, I wonder whether many governments of the modern world could be described as peacemakers? Pope John Paul II said this:

> Let us not accept violence as the way of peace. Let us instead begin by respecting true freedom: the resulting peace will be able to satisfy the world's expectations, for it will be a peace built on justice, a peace founded on the incomparable dignity of the free human being.

It's easier, or at least more comfortable, to answer such a question impersonally. I can criticize the government. I can point out their faults. But am I a peacemaker – do I respect the dignity of the true human being? Do I bring people together or push them apart? Do my lifestyle and my choices create a neighbourhood where people can be at peace with one another? Do I even know the names of my neighbours, the needs of my work colleagues? Peacemaking is not just down to governments; it is down to me.

I like to believe that people in the long run are going to do more to promote peace than our governments. Indeed, I think that people want peace so much that one of these days governments had better get out of the way and let them have it.[24]

Yet if I know my own weaknesses as well as the weaknesses of others, I am brought to a place where I realize not only the value of other people, but I am convinced that we *need* each other. Peacemaking is not just about avoiding conflict. It is about *building a better world*. It is about building a common purpose, recognizing common worth, identifying common goals. This principle means that we do not just recognize the value of one another, we recognize the *need* of one another. The world will not be a better place *unless* there are other people, different to me, in it. We need each other; we need people of difference in order to create a better world. Moshe Dayan, the Israeli general and politician, was right – if we want to make peace we must learn to talk to our enemies as well as to our friends. Whether the tension we are trying to overcome is one caused by poverty or one caused by cultural, racial or religious difference, we will never build a better world unless we can listen to and learn from one another.

## Principle 8: Opposition to such a lifestyle is guaranteed, but it will not defeat this lifestyle

*Blessed are those who are persecuted because of righteousness, for theirs is the Kingdom of Heaven.*

And so the last principle of the beatitudes connects us to the first in the promise that Jesus makes. Let's just recap on the principles that I've pulled out of what Jesus said thus far. My suggestion is that these principles articulate a Christian spirituality that helps to build a better world:

1. Poor people matter and God is on their side.
2. Grief and pain may be a part of life, but there is hope.

24. Dwight D. Eisenhower (US President and General, 1890–1969).

71

3. Power will be given to those who should have it.
4. Striving for justice in the world is a good thing to do and it will eventually work.
5. Compassionate action evokes compassionate response.
6. All of us have faults, but we can all reach our God-given potential.
7. Peacemaking is vital and reflects God's heart.

No wonder this last principle gives hope to those that will face opposition! Employing these principles in their actions and attitudes would have meant certain opposition for first-century followers of Jesus. Both the religious and the political authorities would have struggled to deal with such revolutionary thinking. Here was a view of the world that was not based on power, or prestige or position. It was not based on heritage or wealth or influence. Instead it was a set of principles deeply rooted in God's view of people. These principles were certain to lead to opposition then, and they are certain to lead to opposition now.

This points to an ideology for action and change that is beyond political affiliation, beyond nationality and even beyond religious preferences. Here are a set of values, a set of principles that are deeply rooted in a relationship with the truth that could transform individuals, communities and society as a whole. But we shouldn't expect people to applaud such an approach. It undermines the base of power for Religion and for politics as it has come to be in the Western world. It points to the individual, and in particular to the oppressed individual, and says that they matter and that they are of equal value, worth and significance to you or me. It suggests that change will only come with justice and respect and love. It points to the need of difference and others. It demolishes insularity and individualism but respects the rights of all. It suggests that there is as much wrong with me that needs to be fixed as there is with you. It cries out that war and violence do not work – they never have and they never will.

It is no wonder, therefore, that Jesus promises the same thing in this last beatitude as he did in the first – God is with you when you live like this. He is on your side. The reason for that is simple – when you live like this you are living the way Jesus lived.

## Conclusion

It is from the numberless diverse acts of courage and belief that human history is shaped. Each time a man stands up for an ideal or acts to improve the lot of others or strikes out against injustice, he sends forth a tiny ripple of hope, and crossing each other from a million different centers of energy and daring, those ripples build a current that can sweep down the mightiest walls of oppression and resistance.[25]

I have tried to show how the coherence for a Christian spirituality that builds a better world could come from the principles outlined in the beatitudes at the beginning of the Sermon on the Mount. There are many more principles that could be pulled from the Sermon on the Mount, or from the life and example of Jesus. Reflection, dependence upon God, generosity, graciousness and forgiveness are just a few. Time and space doesn't enable us to explore them all. What excites me most is the possibility that the principles I have articulated might just resonate with you. Whether or not you are a follower of Christ, you may have just read some of the guiding principles for your own life. They may have provided you with the charter that you need to join up some disparate commitments and priorities in your life. That is a good thing. At the same time, I have begun to set the compass correctly. What I want to do is show that Christian spirituality makes sense of the world. The principles it adheres to, and there are so many more than I have articulated here, are relevant and credible. They make a difference in the world. They are tough! They demand our lives, our energy and our commitment. Even if a few of them are principles that you are already trying to live by, then you will know that. But they are worth it!

In the next chapter we will look at some of the key things that Christian faith leads to in some specific areas of public life, but for now I just want to make the point that God is with us when we are

25. Robert F. Kennedy.

with the poor, building a better world. Let me leave you with a thought from Bono:

> God is in the slums, in the cardboard boxes where the poor play house. God is in the silence of a mother who has infected her child with a virus that will end both their lives. God is in the cries heard under the rubble of war. God is in the debris of wasted opportunity and lives, and God is with us if we are with them.[26]

---

26. Bono, keynote address to the National Prayer Breakfast, 2 February 2006, Washington DC.

# Positively Christian

# 4

*What does Christian faith believe in?*

> The whole world is upside down because it puts economics before the human and social needs of people. We need to have different rules.[1]

> Now as never before, we have within our grasp the means to eliminate abject poverty once and for all.[2]

I've tried to make a strong case for an understanding of Christian faith that sees it as a positive motivator for change on both a personal and a communal level. In the last two chapters we've explored some pretty important challenges and principles. From the charter given in Chapter 3[3] we've begun to unpack some of

---

1. Taken from Robert Kennedy's Address to the University of Capetown, South Africa on the Day of Affirmation, 6 June 1966. For further details of the speech, see http://www.rfkmemorial.org/lifevision/dayofaffirmation/.
2. Gordon Brown, UK Chancellor of the Exchequer.
3. Once again, if you need a reminder of the elements of the charter given in Chapter 3, then here are the eight basic points I made:
   1. Poor people matter and God is on their side.
   2. Grief and pain may be part of life, but there is hope.
   3. Power will be given to those who should have it.
   4. Striving for justice in the world is a good thing to do and it will eventually work.
   5. Compassionate action evokes compassionate response.
   6. All of us have faults, but we can all reach our God-given potential.
   7. Peacemaking is vital and reflects God's heart.
   8. Opposition to such a lifestyle is guaranteed, but it will not defeat this lifestyle.

the foundational principles that lie behind Christian faith and lead to an engaged and positive view of the world. We'll continue that journey here by trying to outline some of the positive principles of Christian faith.

## Perception and honesty

To speak of Christian faith as *positive* and *engaged* is to swim against the tide of public opinion and perception. Unfortunately, Christians have not always done a great job of helping people understand who we are and what we believe in. Perhaps some of us who call ourselves followers of Christ have reflected him badly. It is possible that the Church has created misunderstanding in the first place. I think all those who follow Christ have a responsibility here – so I want to issue a plea. If you are reading these words and you are already trying to live according to the example and life of Christ would you join me in a lifelong commitment to give an honest reflection of the God that we serve? When we see God maligned, caricatured and misrepresented by those who share our faith, I think we should say something! We need to stand up for our positive and compassionate and caring God, but we need to do so graciously and lovingly.

Honest critique is helpful; angry, bitter words and reactions are not. Followers of Christ might misrepresent him and Christian values – but in making that assertion I am placing *myself* firmly in the same category. I am part of the problem as well as being committed to becoming part of the solution. It is not my intention to detail the errors, mistakes and caricatures of Christian faith that exist in the minds of many people. I acknowledge that they exist and apologize for the ways in which I perpetuate those misconceptions. At the same time, I want to articulate and celebrate ten areas in which I think Christian faith can make a positive contribution to the communities of which we are a part. I'm not going to look at each one in detail. Instead, I want to introduce the principle, unpack it a little and then move on. My aim is to create a sense of momentum with these principles that will help us to understand the broad sweep of how Christian faith contributes to building a better world.

## 1. Human dignity matters

On 10 December 1948, the Universal Declaration of Human Rights stated in its preamble:

> Whereas recognition of the inherent dignity and of the equal and inalienable rights of all members of the human family is the foundation of freedom, justice and peace in the world.[4]

Article 1 of the declaration states:

> All human beings are born free and equal in dignity and rights. They are endowed with reason and conscience and should act towards one another in a spirit of brotherhood.

This Universal Declaration was also recognized and built upon by the European Convention on Human Rights on 4 November 1950 in Rome and its five subsequent protocols that acknowledge and seek to protect the rights of all people.[5]

The United Kingdom does not have a written constitution but deeply embedded within the governance structures, legislation and societal norms of the UK is an inherent commitment to the principle of the dignity of every human life. The UK also recognizes the European Convention on Human Rights and introduced the Human Rights Act in 1998.

The Human Rights movement itself is not a 21st-century invention, however. The dignity of all people has a deep connection not only to humanitarian and secular thinking in the 20th

---

4. For more information and the full text of the Universal Declaration of Human Rights see http://www.un.org/Overview/rights.html.
5. The European Convention on Human Rights was introduced in Rome on 4 November 1950. Its five protocols were introduced in Paris on 20 March 1952; Strasbourg on 6 May 1963 (two protocols), 16 September 1963, 20 January 1966. For more information see http://www.hri.org/docs/ECHR50.html#C.Preamble.

century, but also to the evolved thinking and attitudes of people over a great many centuries. The United States of America is founded as a nation upon the central premises of the equality of all people. Almost any American will tell you that their great nation was birthed in a longing for equality and justice – indeed most of them would be able to recite to you these famous words from the Declaration of Independence:

> We hold these truths to be self-evident, that all men are created equal, that they are endowed by their Creator with certain unalienable Rights, that among these are Life, Liberty and the pursuit of Happiness.[6]

Human dignity is a principle that moves us to action, the dignity of the rich and the poor, of men and women, of young and old, of black and white. This inherent recognition of the equal worth and value of all people is perhaps the most often referred to 'ideal' and the least lived out. We often forget that in the USA and the UK the commitment to human worth and dignity has its roots in the Christian understanding of personhood. It is the faith conviction that all people are equal that was at the basis of the desire for people to be treated fairly. This conviction fundamentally opposes the idea that some people are better than others. It is the ultimate leveller. If truly embraced and lived out it would be the greatest single source of transformation in attitudes that the world has ever seen.

From the very opening pages of the Christian and Jewish Bible to the example and life of Christ, the principle of equality has been articulated clearly. Indeed, it is this fundamentally Christian and Jewish principle that has acted as the bedrock for much of modern thinking about human beings. I am not suggesting that other faiths deny the equality of human beings and the dignity of all people, but Christian faith goes further than all of them. The fundamentally positive contribution to society that Christianity makes is that *every* human being bears God's image and *every* human being is given life by God. Irrespective of their colour, their sexual

---

6. The American Declaration of Independence was signed on 4 July 1776. For more information see http://www.ushistory.org/declaration/document/index.htm.

preferences, their gender, their religion or their creed, Christianity believes that *all people* are equal. It is contained within the older and newer sections of the Christian Bible[7] and is exhibited across the history of the Christian Church. Jesus' own example of mixing with the socially excluded and the downtrodden was a clear example and message that he saw worth and value in all people, and honoured the image of his father in all.

Consider St Francis of Assisi, a 13th-century monk who served the poor and the destitute, and Mother Teresa of Calcutta in the 20th century. These followers of Christ gave their lives to those in need as a service to the world and to the God they worshipped. Throughout two millennia, countless Christians, motivated by the commitment to serve other human beings, have given their time, their money, their lives and their passions to care for others. I am not suggesting for one moment that governments and societies get this right! One only has to look at the deep injustices of Northern Ireland or of the civil rights struggles in the US to see that there is much that still needs to change. The travesty of the poor (and largely black) communities of New Orleans seemingly being abandoned by the federal government following the devastation of hurricane Katrina in 2005 is a modern-day blight on US attitudes and a reminder that this principle is not being implemented as well as it could be. The same is true of the way the UK government has treated asylum seekers in recent years. Both in the US and the UK, the fear of public opinion has caused both governments to be weak rather than strong in the face of the challenge of truly respecting all people. The global struggle with death, disease and poverty is also a stark reminder that as world nations, we are not

7. Remember the Christian 'Old Testament' is actually the Jewish Bible and I would prefer to call it the Older Testament of Christian Scripture. Read the first chapter of the first book in the Bible (Genesis 1.27) for a staggering statement about the equality of people. Also read through Psalm 139 that is part of a collection of songs, laments and poems written by Jews. In the Newer Testament, letters written by the Apostle Paul to encourage early followers of Christ pick up the same theme of human dignity – particularly one he wrote to followers of Christ in an area called Colossae. The book is called 'Colossians' in the Newer Testament and chapter 3 is particularly interesting.

getting this right, as is the heart-breaking reality of the existence of human trafficking on a massive scale across the world.[8]

I acknowledge the fact that the Church has not always been good at defending human rights. I am as embarrassed by that as are many other followers of Christ. However, the point I am making is a simple one. Christian faith affirms the dignity of all people and the equality of all people. You do not have to be a follower of Christ to share that value. But the value itself *is a positive Christian value* about society, life and how we relate to one another. I know this for certain: where one person is treated as more important than another, or one person's preferences are seen as more significant than the preferences of another, whatever the name given to society, it is *not* a Christian society. Christian faith upsets the comfort zone of those who talk about human rights and it demands that the conversations are turned into actions. It is not possible, within the parameters of Christian faith, simply to acknowledge that human rights are important. The acknowledgement in the head of a follower of Christ that all people are equal must result in changed behaviour and changed attitudes. Anything less is hypocrisy.

> For me as a Christian one of the most important of these teachings is contained in the parable of the Good Samaritan, when Jesus answers the question 'who is my neighbour'. It is a timeless story of a victim of a mugging who was ignored by his own countrymen but helped by a foreigner – and a despised foreigner at that. The implication drawn by Jesus is clear. Everyone is our neighbour, no matter what race, creed or colour. The need to look after a fellow human being is far more important than any cultural or religious differences.[9]

Florence Nightingale, the mother of modern nursing, profoundly understood the dignity of human beings. Her vision of nursing grew out of a profound faith in God that rooted and grounded her

---

8. For more information on how to do something about human trafficking see www.stopthetraffik.org.
9. Queen Elizabeth II, Christmas message, 2004.

life. She had a powerful sense of God's directing her toward nursing at least four times in her life and she eventually gave up a comfortable and wealthy lifestyle to pursue what she considered to be her vocation. She travelled to the Crimea, working in terrible squalor and horrendous conditions as she cared for the dying and the sick. Amidst the filth and pain of war, she saw the dignity of the soldiers. She sensed that she was living out the biblical commandment of love, caring for brutalized and traumatized soldiers. She refused to see these men as animals, choosing instead to see the image of God in them and to respond to that truth:

> In this she encompassed the whole moral basis for care. From these beginnings grew her own understanding of God's relationship to human beings and the implication of this for nursing. She spent her life exploring this theology in complex and often muddled writing, but also putting it into practical action through the nurses that trained in her name and with her principles.[10]

## 2. Justice should be a priority

Deeply embedded within a Christian understanding of the world is a longing for justice. Saint Augustine is attributed as having said that charity is no substitute for justice withheld. In fact it could be said that justice is the cry of God through the Hebrew Bible and the New Testament. It is a longing for justice that drives the calls for reformation in the context of the Jewish people and their journey through exile and into their homeland in the first five or six hundred years of the existence of the people of Israel. One central figure in the Hebrew Bible is the prophet Micah who declares that the only thing that is required of those who claim to follow God is to act justly, love mercy and walk humbly before

---

10. Taken from *The Historical Tradition of Care* by Ann Bradshaw, in *Caring: The Compassion and Wisdom of Nursing* edited by Gosia Brykczynska (London: Arnold, 1996), chapter 2.

God.[11] Repeatedly within the context of the Bible God calls those who claim to follow him to act in a just way. They are to stand with the poor, to care for the sick, to welcome those who are asylum seekers, to share the benefit of their wealth. Deeply embedded within the culture of the Jewish nation was the demand that they were to be fair with one another, to develop a social system that did not oppress others or take them for granted or manipulate them.

Indeed, what set the early nation of Israel apart from many other ethnic groups in the Near and Middle East was their deep commitment to fairness and equality. These same commitments are carried into the early Christian community, where wealth was shared and where those who were in need were tended. In fact, the early followers of Christ are often referred to as those who shared their goods amongst the community. The great parable of Jesus concerning the Samaritan[12] shows us that Jesus taught that we had a responsibility and a commitment to justice for those we come into contact with. Not only that, but the attitude of Jesus to those who oppressed others is deeply challenging.

This commitment to justice is also unpacked in the previous chapter, but it is enough to say here that the building of a better world will never happen without a deeper and stronger commitment to issues of justice. We cannot change the world just by helping those who need our help – we must also ask the difficult questions about why they ended up in the situations they did in the first place. Christian faith calls for a change not only in the lives of individuals, but also in the behaviour and attitudes of nations and societies. The biblical picture of a just welfare system, for example, includes:

- enabling and maintaining household self-reliance where possible
- maintaining personal dignity
- emphasis on prevention of crisis and poverty

11. A prophet in this sense is not just someone who foretells the future, but someone who communicates God's heart on issues that people are facing. See Micah, chapter 6, particularly verse 8.
12. This is recorded in the Gospel of Luke, chapter 10.

- the duty of care of the individual, the extended family, the local community and the king (government).[13]

Justice, for the Christian, never happens in isolation. It is deeply connected to our understanding of individuals, families, society, political structures, government, possessions and international relations. Justice, for the follower of Christ, is as much a *relational* issue as it is a political one.

At the heart of authentic Christian spirituality, then, lies not just a commitment to treat people with dignity and acknowledge their equality, but also the commitment to fight injustice, to overcome exclusion and to ensure a fairer, better world. And this is not the job of the state only, or the power brokers; it is the job of every individual. We bring justice to the world by challenging the systems of injustice that exist and by living just lives ourselves.

## 3. We are committed to service

Christian faith is not about power: it never has been. So the third positive principle of Christian faith is the principle of service. Christian faith forces those who seek to live out its principles to care for and think about others. This is sacrificial, and it is transformative. Again, the example of Christ is both deeply challenging, and inspiring, when we consider these principles. In him we see acceptance and service – even of those who most deeply rejected him. This principle of service is married to commitment and is a deeply positive contribution to society.

Christian organizations are massively involved in acts of kindness and compassion locally, regionally, nationally and internationally. Their service is often underfunded and overlooked. In many situations their faith distinctive has proven a barrier to help and support from government bodies – a discriminatory practice which must surely be challenged and ended. Yet these committed

13. These ideas are unpacked in the excellent book: *Jubilee Manifesto: A Framework, Agenda and Strategy for Christian Social Reform* edited by Michael Schluter and John Ashcroft (Leicester: IVP, 2005), pp. 178–86.

followers of Christ continue to make a difference. They embody the deeply challenging words of a figure from the Older Testament – the prophet Isaiah:[14]

> Break the chains of injustice ...
> Get rid of exploitation in the workplace ...
> Free the oppressed ...
> Cancel debts ...
> Sharing your food with the hungry ...
> Inviting the homeless poor into your homes ...
> Putting clothes on the shivering ill-clad ...
> Being available to your own families ...
> Being generous with the hungry ...
> Giving yourselves to the down and out ...

One example of this selfless approach to service and compassion is shown in the Simple Way Community that lives and works in Philadelphia. The community seeks to serve those in need and to demonstrate God's heart of compassion, justice and mercy for people. They live in community, share their possessions, time and lives and operate a number of different projects and programmes to help those in need. From gardening to T-shirt making, this community of twelve people or so is having a massive impact on the people they serve. But above their programmes and their projects, they simply love and serve others. This can be demonstrated by the commitment of the Simple Way to serve those who arrive on their doorstep needing help. They seek to offer shelter to those who need a home and a meal to those who are hungry. They are an open and welcome community who provide a place for people simply to 'be'. They do what they believe Jesus would do – and it is working.[15]

The Simple Way are choosing to live out their service and love in community, but there are hundreds of thousands of followers of

14. For the full text of this take a few moments to read Isaiah, chapter 58.
15. For more information see their website www.thesimpleway.org. Shane Claiborne is a member of the community and has written a book that unpacks some of the principles behind this group of fellow travellers. *The Irresistible Revolution: Living as an Ordinary Radical* (Grand Rapids: Zondervan, 2005).

Christ who choose to run and help in kids' clubs, youth clubs, soup kitchens and homelessness projects. There are more involved in teaching, school governorship and healthcare. Add to that the thousands of volunteers, helpers and workers who commit their time and energy to their community either through centrally run initiatives or through things that will never be labelled 'Christian' and you begin to get a picture of a rich and varied tapestry of activity which is serving others. To quote someone whose writing and communication I have enjoyed:

> These are the kind of people who change the world. They improvise and adapt and innovate and explore new ways to get things done. They don't make a lot of noise, and they don't draw a lot of attention to themselves.[16]

Long after government's funding streams have stopped and the latest idea about neighbourhood renewal has changed, you will still find followers of Christ committed to their communities and committed to others. That is because that commitment springs from a deep commitment to love and to serve others. They do not do what they do for recognition, for power or for influence. Followers of Christ serve because they know it is how to live. This is even more than just a 'principle'. It is a necessity of living the way Jesus lived. Such heroes do not want the applause of the world, or even the applause of heaven. Their reward is seeing hope and life and joy in the eyes of those they serve. That is enough.

Those who argue for approaches to building a better world that suggest that it can be bought or forced into being have not lived long enough with those in need. The idea that throwing money at a community will change it is both naïve and ineffective. In order to see change we must become change. This example of service

16. Rob Bell leads a group of people following Christ in Grand Rapids, Michigan. The Community is called 'Mars Hill', taken from a story of the early church in the New Testament called the Book of Acts. In it, the Apostle Paul finds a group of people in Athens at a place called Mars Hill who are standing at an altar to the unknown God. Paul engages positively with them. Rob has written a fantastic book that tells the story of what he thinks are the important bits of Christian faith. See *Velvet Elvis: Repainting the Christian Faith* by Rob Bell (Grand Rapids: Zondervan, 2005), p. 168.

and devotion and love is perfectly demonstrated in Christ, who
came to serve.

## 4. Being part of a community is central

> All mankind is of one author, and is one volume; when one
> man dies, one chapter is not torn out of the book, but translated
> into a better language; and every chapter must be so
> translated ... As therefore the bell that rings to a sermon, calls
> not upon the preacher only, but upon the congregation to
> come: so this bell calls us all: but how much more me, who am
> brought so near the door by this sickness ... No man is an
> island, entire of itself ... any man's death diminishes me,
> because I am involved in mankind; and therefore never send to
> know for whom the bell tolls; it tolls for thee.[17]

John Donne's famous meditation on the interconnectedness of all
humanity was written in the wake of a great deal of pain and
suffering as the Black Death gripped London. His words articulate
the Christian principle of community. In an age of isolationism and
individualism, the spiritual commitment to community at the heart
of Christian faith is a strong reminder of our need for one another.
It may seem strange to place such a principle in a list of the positive
contributions that Christian faith brings to building a better world,
but let me explain why I think it is so important.

If I live my life in isolation from others, according to my own
preferences, ideas and concepts, I cut myself off from the opportunity to learn, to change, to be changed and to become a fuller,
more balanced human being. I am part of the created order of this
whole planet. Donne's words are not simply poetic; they are true. I
am diminished when I live in isolation from my community. Not
only that, my community is also diminished when I 'opt out'. I am

17. John Donne, *Meditation XVII*.

lessened and the community is lessened.[18] The biblical encouragement to live as part of a believing community is clear, but there is also a call for us to live as part of the geographic and social communities of which we are part. I am like a pinch of salt in my community. I flavour it in a particular way and give it a distinctiveness. I am a light in my community, giving it a distinctive blend of the spectrum of colour. In the same way others in my community – whether socially or geographically – flavour and illuminate my life in a particular way.[19]

This is a spiritual truth that goes back to the fundamental assertion of Christian faith that we are created to live and dwell in community. We need one another. In an interview with Diana, Princess of Wales for the BBC documentary programme, *Panorama*, she said this:

> There is no better way to dismantle a personality than to isolate it.[20]

The reality of our need for other people is probably something that is not new to you, but the lack of connectedness with others is nevertheless a very worrying trait of modern life. Against this backdrop, Christian spirituality is not an individual activity. The need for others – the need for the challenge of others as well as the blessing – is central. From a selfish point of view I *cannot* become all that I can be unless I am in connection with others.

Yet I recognize that Christian communities are not always good at connecting, or at creating a sense of community. We can struggle with creating a sense of community within the context of those that we know, let alone trying to build a sense of community with those we do not know. The latter seems to me to be a major

18. Although it is true that the Christian faith community needs all those who are part of it to play their part, this is not what I am talking about here. Rather, I am discussing the fact that society as a whole needs me and I need other members of society. My geographic community is weakened if I live there but isolate myself from it.

19. These images of salt and light are not my own. Instead they are taken from the same sermon that I focused on in Chapter 3 – the Sermon on the Mount. See Matthew 5.13–16 for more details.

20. As quoted in John Burke, *No Perfect People Allowed: Creating a Come as You Are Culture in the Church* (Grand Rapids: Zondervan, 2005), p. 267.

contribution that we can make to community life, however. We need to celebrate this counter-cultural aspect of our character and our spirituality. But that demands a different understanding of other people. If we see others in our communities as infringements of our space and time we will never grasp the idea of true community. If we see those that we seek to help as clients rather than people, we stifle our own ability to function as well as theirs. Christian spirituality recognizes that in any exchange the flow moves both ways. So when we campaign to end world poverty something also happens to us. When we march to tell governments that injustice is wrong, we march *in step* with others and we are also changed. Community strengthens us and strengthens others – but only when we enter into it.

Community helps us to grow and develop our own sense of spirituality and purpose too. There are some assumptions that we need to challenge if this is true. For example, spiritual growth and development is not linear; instead it is shaped by encounters and unexpected twists and turns in the road of our lives and experience. Not only that, but as we live as parts of communities we soon realize that development in our own lives is not necessarily matched by increasing certainty. Development of our own lives and self-understanding might lead to a greater sense of dependency and tangible *inability* to answer some questions: it is only in community that we can find safety for this kind of rather chaotic journey. Furthermore, as we grow and develop, we may find that our lives get *worse* rather than better. Ironically, building a better world means that our own assumptions must be challenged and some of those challenges will mean that we no longer see some elements of our lives as 'good' or 'best' in the way that we once did. For example, our financial security might be put into question as we seek to build a better world because being part of a community has changed our perspective on the personal procurement of wealth. What is clear is this – human and spiritual development cannot only be individualistic.[21]

21. To unpack some of these themes see Tim Conder, *The Church in Transition: The Journey of Existing Churches into the Emerging Culture* (Grand Rapids: Zondervan, 2005), pp. 100–121.

## 5. Inclusion and diversity are fundamental priorities

Inclusion is fundamentally the approach of counting others in rather than counting them out[22] and it lies at the heart of Christian spirituality. The Church was never supposed to be a group of people who existed for their own benefit. In fact, at the heart of Christian faith is the conviction that God has graciously included us in the great story of life, its purpose and meaning. This fundamental commitment to treat people as part of a community is intrinsic to authentic spirituality. God treats us as 'in' not 'out'. That view, if adopted, would significantly change the way we view others. One of the greatest challenges that many of the people we know face is one of exclusion. They feel like they are not part of the right crowd and that somehow they are supposed to sit on the sidelines of life rather than play a full part. But what if that is wrong?

Christian faith tells me that everyone has a valid contribution to the tapestry of life in a community. What if we change our default mechanism from one of suspicion and self-protection to one of trust and self-giving? Then the poor and the excluded are no longer objects of our compassion or mercy; they are people with whom we spend time, individuals who have as much right to life as I do. That would mean a huge change in our approaches to talking about the problems in our society and our world. From self-protecting trade policies to the imposition of local spending budgets on hospitals, schools and communities, inclusion would change the way we do things. Instead of imposing, we would dialogue. Instead of winning an argument we might just have a conversation where there are no winners or losers, just people who learn from each other.

You cannot explore Christian spirituality without addressing the question of inclusion. There are some members of the world-wide Christian community who are exclusive in their approach. They will only work with those who agree with them. They see their primary aim as making other people believe the same thing as they

22. For more on this whole idea of inclusion see Steve Chalke and Anthony Watkis, *Intelligent Church: A Journey toward Christ Centered Community* (Grand Rapids: Zondervan, 2006), pp. 31–47.

do and live in the same way that they live. There are others who disagree with such an approach, however. They see themselves as *inclusive*. Their view is that because of their Christian spirituality they must embrace and work with others. I would include myself in their number. We do not understand how you can claim to have a Christian spirituality while at the same time acting in an exclusive or discriminatory way to others. For those of us who hold such a view, our spirituality of *inclusion* is what sets us apart from those who see their central aim as making other people like us. Inclusion means we serve all. We do not exclude, we do not reject, we do not close the door. We embrace, we do not just welcome. To have such an attitude of inclusion means that we *must* serve, we *must* engage. For us, engagement is to inclusion as *action* is to *attitude*.

I don't think we should take this too lightly. Inclusion means that we will explore different ways of approaching those in need. We will work with them, not for them. We will focus more on advocacy and empowerment than we do on control and lobbying. The Disability Rights Movement has a phrase that might help us understand what I am trying to say here. It is simply this – *Nothing for us without us*. Maybe inclusion means that we need to stop doing *to* people and start doing *with* them. Maybe, just maybe, an inclusive approach to building a better world would mean an entirely different understanding of politics, power and community transformation. Maybe it would change our attitudes in our families and in our places of work – because we count people in before we count them out. We approach others with open hands rather than clenched fists.

An inclusive approach does not mean a one-size-fits-all approach, however. Rather, it celebrates diversity and difference. It does not demand that we find the lowest common denominator. Instead, it welcomes and celebrates difference because it sees strength in difference. Diversity can lead to breakdown if we allow it to become prejudice. However, Christian spirituality allows no room for prejudicial behaviour. Diversity strengthens a community; it allows room for new experiences, new ideas and new encounters. Christian faith does not 'tolerate' difference, it welcomes it. Once again, this is not something that we are necessarily always good at, but authentic spirituality that flows from Christian faith is one that welcomes difference and helps people to find their place and flourish in it.

Diversity does not mean that there has to be endorsement of all things, however. Diversity can only flourish when distinctiveness is recognized. I have not sought to articulate the worldviews of other religions because I am not a member of another faith. As a follower of Christ, I am able to celebrate the rich contribution that those of another faith and those of none make to society. I have a duty to respect them, but I do not have to endorse all they believe. Where there is common ground, I must find that common ground. Where there is difference, I must allow for that difference and celebrate it where celebration is possible. Where differences are deep, respect must be deeper still. It is only as respect and trust flourish that diversity and inclusion can grow. I am absolutely convinced that when it comes to building a better world, the various faiths of the world have a massive amount upon which we can agree. It is the duty of those who have faith to find common ground and work out how we build together. Our commitment to build together must also be accompanied by a willingness to be clear about our own distinctiveness, however. Perhaps we must move from confrontation to dialogue. Arguing hasn't got us very far – perhaps it never will.[23]

## 6. A holistic approach is the only one that works

We are whole units. Christian spirituality recognizes the connectedness of all of life. We cannot build a better world by approaching life as if it is lived in 'little boxes';[24] our physical, social and material worlds are deeply connected. In its worst form, Christian faith has separated out spiritual life from material life – this has little to do with authentic faith. The fact that you are reading this book and have survived this far suggests that you really

23. Joy Madeiros has done a great deal of work investigating and articulating the idea of distinctiveness in faith issues. She is contactable via Faithworks by emailing info@faithworks.info.
24. Remember Chapter 1 and Pete Seeger's song.

understand this principle. Your commitment to building a better world is driven not just by the desire to see material change. You will probably also want to see social change; a change in attitudes and hearts as well as in physical situations. You have already been practising the holistic approach that I am suggesting has a strong connection to Christian spirituality.

Changing the house a person lives in will not in and of itself change the person. They may still have their own struggles and difficulties and insecurities that they know they need to deal with. I can tell someone they can change until I am blue in the face, but they will not change until they choose to. Our health, our attitudes, our physical and emotional states are all linked. Christian spirituality recognizes this deep connection. It not only recognizes this, it celebrates it. It celebrates it because authentic Christian spirituality sees the 'goodness' of the created world as well as the 'goodness' of life itself and the diversity of relationships and emotions that we experience. The spiritual and the physical are two sides of the same coin to the follower of Christ. Understanding holism means we recognize that poverty is a spiritual issue as well as a physical one. Injustice is a spiritual issue as well as a physical one. Houses, cars, finances and family – how we think about all of these things is as much about our spiritual attitudes as it is our social and physical ones. This is an important contribution to the discussion about how we might build a better world. It is important because if a holistic understanding of life is a right understanding, then service provision, politics, community development, healthcare, education, housing and a whole list of other things become *both* spiritual and material issues.

That's a pretty dramatic change in understanding. My own view is that the holistic understanding of life and community that Christian spirituality brings to contemporary culture is a much-needed correction to the boxed, silo-mentalities that we can often encounter. At the same time, I think it will take some time to move beyond the language of holism and get to the reality of thinking holistically. I think those of us who are followers of Christ and have grasped holism can be of great benefit here – but we must be willing to be of benefit. We must be willing to engage if we are to see change.

## 7. Participation is empowerment

Christian spirituality is committed to the principle that every contribution is meaningful. So often, particularly amongst those working for social change from a non-governmental or voluntary perspective, there can be a sense of frustration that those 'in power' are shaping the destinies of those who are not. Those of us who try to influence government and policy can become enraged at the sense of dismissal we sometimes feel. Yet at the heart of Christian faith is the fundamental conviction that change can only happen when everyone is involved and when we recognize that all of those contributors bring something unique and valuable to the change process. The work of the volunteer really is as valuable and life changing as the work of the Chief Executive or the politician.

In Chapter 1, I articulated the views of faith held by the population, pop stars and politicians. I did so not just because I was looking for some alliteration to make the words sound good on the page. Rather, I wanted to make the point that the views of the individual who is little known are as important as the views of those who are in the spotlight. Faithworks,[25] the movement I have the privilege of leading, is built around this principle. The thousands of members of the Faithworks Movement are each committed to social change. It is *together* that they form the movement. Some of those involved in the movement spend millions of pounds on making the world a better place and have worked in many countries. Others are committed to being good parents and neighbours and would never dream of millions of dollars or pounds being spent on something. They would see that as way beyond their contribution. The strength of the movement, however, is that both the individual who is passionate about change in their street and the global organization that is committed to the erad-ication of poverty and HIV/AIDS are needed to make this movement authentic.

Furthermore, I believe the Christian underpinning of social transformation works alongside those of other faiths and those of no faith. I am convinced that *together* we can build a better world.

25. For more information on Faithworks see www.faithworks.info and the Appendix at the end of this book.

Alone, we will have limited success – but working in partnership with one another we truly can change the world. Christian spirituality allows for and welcomes that sense of participation that is not gauged by external factors. It welcomes the administrator, the volunteer and the leader, and it values the small acts of kindness in the same way as it celebrates the large and grand gestures and programmes.

Individuals who work in isolation from one another will not change the world. Christian communities with silo-mentalities will not change it. Politicians who ignore the voluntary sector or exploit the faith sector will not change it. Business will not change the world either. Charity will not change the world. Trade justice on its own will not change the world. Full church buildings will not change the world. People from different backgrounds, with different ideas, but with a common commitment to one another and a shared desire to make things better might just make a difference. To recognize and enable the full participation of all who want to be involved in building a better world is the greatest form of empowerment possible.

## 8. Involvement means sacrifice

I cannot explore the positive principles of Christian spirituality in the world without acknowledging the cross. For followers of Christ, it is a potent symbol of suffering, pain, and ultimate triumph. While there are many, many interpretations of the meaning of the cross, none of them contains the whole truth about the way in which the cross redeems the world. As a follower of Christ, I think it is vital that we avoid the deep mistake of divorcing the cross and its meaning from the rest of the life, example and message of Christ. Christian spirituality cannot ignore the cross: it stands as a symbol of the pain of involvement in the world. To commit to our own transformation, God paid the ultimate price: Jesus laid down his life on the cross for the world. The cross is the place at which the ultimate cost of human selfishness is paid. We cannot 'relive' the cross. It is God's unique word to deal with the pain and wrong and evil in our world. Without it – without Christ, there is no hope.

However, there is a sense in which the cross is an example for those who want to see genuine transformation and change in the world around them. Christian spirituality does not believe that changing the world is easy, cheap or detached from personal commitment. The cross reminds us of this. Whether you are a follower of Christ or not, the cross can make sense of the pain and the suffering that you experience as you seek to see change. It somehow helps to know that pain and opposition, and perhaps the ultimate price that is giving our lives for a better world, is part of the deal. The world will not be changed by half-hearted commitment; instead it will take our lives. The cross is a reminder of that and a pointer that helps us through the pain to see the positive impact on a world in need. Yet we also see and understand in the cross that this pain is personal as well as corporate. For it to affect the world, it must affect you. For the cross to have power to change the world, it must change us. Without the seamless messages of the incarnation, the cross and the resurrection, Christian spirituality would not be complete.

The cross, seen within the context of the whole life and ministry of Christ, also leads us to the next two principles.

## 9. God is intrinsically involved in the world he made

It is easy to believe that the fight against injustice and poverty cannot be won. Sometimes, those of us who are engaged in the process of challenging injustice can become so caught up in the pressure and the pain of those around us that we begin to lose sight of the bigger picture. We fall into the trap of thinking that *we* must change the world. Somehow we become the central force for change in the world. It is here that Christian spirituality has a massive contribution to make because it *knows* that God has not abandoned the world he has made. He is intrinsically involved. Let me try to speak to this principle from a personal perspective.

I could not do what I do if I did not know that God was with me. I have the utmost admiration for those who think that their efforts alone can change the world. I salute their commitment, their zeal and their energy, but I disagree with their understanding.

Like many reading these words, I have known the joy of seeing real change as people have found one another and worked together for the common good. I have celebrated victories over cruel landlords, cancellations of unjust debts, educational achievements by those who have been told they are stupid and changes in policy brought about by good advocacy. However, I have also seen too much pain, despair and recurrent failure to think that the stories of triumph are enough. I have struggled with the pain of helping addicts free themselves of their addiction only to see them succumb to the addiction again.

As a pastor, I have buried too many people who thought they had cracked a habit to believe that human endeavour is enough to bring about change. As part of a geographic community I have seen judgements and policies go the *wrong* way and have become frustrated at the inability of politics to change things on its own. As a human being I have wept at the sheer injustice of the world. As an observer, I have lived through the last third of the 20th century and seen the utter devastation of natural, political and military disasters. A brief reading of the 20th century shows that human beings are not getting better at caring for one another. The optimism of the beginning of the 20th century had dimmed by the beginning of the 21st century. Science may have advanced greatly in the 20th century, but the sense of community, love, support, fairness, justice and equity for which many of us long is no closer now than it was one hundred years ago. The humanist experiment does not appear to be working. In human terms, the ideas of fraternity, liberty and equality are no closer now than they were at the beginning of the French Revolution.

However, as a follower of Christ, I am utterly convinced that God remains intrinsically involved in this world. He is absolutely committed to it. And as I understand and embrace that reality, my understanding of the world itself is changed. The pain I see is not divorced from God; he endures that pain also. I see the small acts of kindness, the tiny breakthroughs and see behind them the same hand and the same force. I am convinced that wherever there is good in the world, wherever justice is done, wherever mercy is experienced, it is a reflection of God's intimate involvement in the world. I see the ultimate Good uniting the acts of those who follow him and those who do not to build a better world. The pain of the world, the distress of the addict, the mistakes of those who have made life-destroying choices are felt and experienced by him. As an individual activist I am bolstered by this faith. I'm certainly confused at times and search for answers, but I also know that he is with me. He has gone ahead of me and he helps me. He is in the eyes of those who are poor and in the pain of those who suffer and in the sight of those who long to make a difference. It is his spirit that I sense when I hear a call for justice – wherever that call for justice comes from and whoever is the speaker.

This conviction keeps me going. It energizes me, that God is the God who is there is what makes all the difference, even if it does not give me the answers I always want. This God is truly called Emmanuel – God with us. And I am utterly, utterly convinced that he is with all those who strive to make the world a better place, whatever their faith, whatever their colour and whatever their motivation.

## 10. There is hope

'Then the prophecies of the old songs have turned out to be true, after a fashion!' said Bilbo.
'Of course!' said Gandalf. 'And why should not they prove true? Surely you don't disbelieve the prophecies, because you had a hand in bringing them about yourself?'
'You don't really suppose, do you, that all your adventures and escapes were managed by mere luck, just for your sole benefit? You are a very fine person, Mr Baggins, and I am very fond of you; but you are only quite a little fellow in the wide world after all.'[26]

Things are not as they will be. In the midst of all the suffering and pain in the world that we experience at this moment in time, the follower of Christ believes that the world will be a just and a fair place. For the follower of Christ, the cry of longing that rises in the

26. *The Hobbit* by J.R.R. Tolkien.

heart of every human being as they see a world in pain is met by a whispered promise from God himself – 'it will not always be this way'. Christian faith is convinced that God will, through the acts of kindness and grace of humanity and through supernatural interventions, make all things right. This is not a pipe-dream for me; it is a promise. It is a promise that I sometimes call to mind with tears flowing down my face and confusion in my heart. Yet it is a promise nevertheless, and it is one that I will not give up.

There is hope not just because we can make a difference. There is hope because God is at work in every act of kindness and mercy. He is the one who will put all things right. The injustice, the pain, the suffering, the poverty and the disjointedness will be rectified. This is a positive principle that pushes me and millions like me to do more, to work harder, to find new ways of caring because as we do, we bring about that change. We bring a better world a little bit closer one act of kindness at a time.

History is not cyclical. It is linear. Things will be put right. That's a promise.

## Making it work

We've explored ten positive principles that Christian spirituality makes in building a better world:

1. Human dignity matters.
2. Justice should be a priority.
3. We are committed to service.
4. Being part of a community is central.
5. Inclusion and diversity are fundamental priorities.
6. A holistic approach is the only one that works.
7. Participation is empowerment.
8. Involvement means sacrifice.
9. God is intrinsically involved in the world he made.
10. There is hope.

These principles, together with the charter of Chapter 3 and the challenges we will explore in Chapters 5 and 6, create a framework for building a better world from a Christian perspective. They provide a clear and connected worldview that makes sense of where we have been, where we are and where we are going. They do not pretend that the world is a better place right now. They do not hide the problems but tackle them head-on. They do not allow anyone to claim that making a difference has nothing to do with them. They acknowledge the reality of injustice, poverty and pain and they give a coherent way forward for dealing with it – for eradicating it. Not only that, they offer a great company of people who are committed to fairness and justice a framework of hope. They lift the heads and the hands of those who long for better. It might be that you have reached this stage of this book and you are one of that number.

Our commitment to changing the world can sometimes drain us. It can suck from our veins the very vitality that motivates us in the first place. We feel like the world cannot or will not change. Perhaps we need to find a worldview that will help us, something that connects the longing in our hearts with the tears in our eyes. My conviction is that Christian faith provides such a worldview. It unites all those who long for a better world. It ties us together. Some of us may be clearer in our understanding of God and his purposes for our lives than others – at least for now. Yet Christian spirituality is an invitation to join the journey. It is the God that made the world inviting us to join him in remaking it. It will take our lives, but that is a good investment, not a bad one. Christian spirituality is at its most authentic and its most effective when it gives purpose to those who live it out. Yet that purpose is neither selfish nor self-centred. The mystery is that the principles we have explored thus far give meaning to our lives, our actions, and our passions *only* as we live our lives for others. It is in seeking to eradicate injustice and poverty and pain that we find ourselves. In challenging injustice we are challenged. In changing the world we are changed. In catching a glimpse of hope in the eyes of someone else we ourselves find hope.

There are a number of ways of 'grounding' all that we have explored. The first is to ask ourselves what kind of community *our* community would become if it were one that embraced the challenges we have explored. What would happen to poverty and injustice in our community if together we approached it as radically as the beatitudes invite? What would happen to our neighbourhood if just a few of those who lived in it sought to model the example and life of Christ with all of its attendant challenges? How would our town change if its leaders were as committed to the positive principles of inclusion, justice and participation as I've set out? I think there would be some radically different neighbourhoods and towns beginning to emerge, don't you? The second way of grounding these challenges is what we now turn to – what does all of this mean for each of us individually? How can we take it seriously as individuals?

# Part III

## Personal Implications?

# How shall we then live?

## Personal implications?

If God exists and if our planet represents God's work of art, we will never grasp why we are here without taking that reality into account.

Assuming with a neutral viewpoint does not change your life — living out a political commitment does. In the same way, the impact of a Christian truth should not be measured by the worth and authority of institutional Christian Religion; it should be measured by the degree of transformation that takes place in the lives of individuals and communities where Christian faith is present. As we have seen, Christian faith can have a transforming impact on communities — but to do so it must first have a transforming influence on our own lives. The author G.K. Chesterton once noted that Christian faith has not been tried and found wanting; rather it has been found difficult and not tried.

As we have already explored, the challenge that lies before those who are motivated to see social, spiritual or societal transformation is to consider where that motivation comes from and having discovered that to live out the implications of their findings honestly and openly. Behind the great monotheistic Religions of the world

1. Philip Yancey, *Prayer: Does It Make Any Difference?* (Grand Rapids: Zondervan, 2009), p. 29.

# How shall we then live?    5

*What role could Christian faith have in my life?*

> If God exists, and if our planet represents God's work of art, we will never grasp why we are here without taking that reality into account.[1]

Agreeing with a political viewpoint does not change your life – living out a political commitment does. In the same way, the impact of Christian faith should not be measured by the wealth and authority of institutional Christian Religion; it should be measured by the degree of transformation that takes place in the lives of individuals and communities where Christian faith is present. As we have seen, Christian faith can have a transforming impact on communities – but to do so it must first have a transforming influence on our own lives. The author G.K. Chesterton once noted that Christian faith has not been tried and found wanting; rather it has been found difficult and not tried.

As we have already explored, the challenge that lies before those who are motivated to see social, spiritual or societal transformation is to consider where that motivation comes from and having discovered that to live out the implications of their findings honestly and openly. Behind the great monotheistic Religions of the world

---

1. Philip Yancey, *Rumours of Another World* (Grand Rapids: Zondervan, 2003), p. 29.

lie central figures. Each contributes and shapes that Religion – so the prophet Mohammed shapes Islam; Abraham shapes Judaism; the ten Gurus are key figures in Sikhism and in Hinduism understanding of God or Brahman is shaped by the teachings and examples of those such as the deities of Krishna, Shiva, Rama and Durga. To understand a particular Religion, we must first take the central figure in that Religion seriously. We must ask ourselves whether their teaching matched their lifestyles and whether their words made sense of their world. We must also ask whether it makes sense of our world today.[2]

At the heart of Christian faith lies Jesus Christ himself. To understand what authentic Christian faith truly is and what it really means for our world and for our lives personally, we must look at Christ and ask the same questions. Does the teaching of Christ match his lifestyle and did it make sense of his world? Does it make sense of our world today? Having done that, we must then make a decision about how we ourselves live.

For all of us, whether we have been following Christ closely or whether we are only beginning the journey, it is important to remember two things. Firstly, none of us gets it right all the time – there are no perfect followers. Secondly, to follow someone is to travel with them and to walk behind them. There is progression and development in Christian faith as there is in any faith. The process of following takes time, patience and commitment. That patience must be demonstrated not only with others but also with ourselves. Perhaps we need to learn not to avoid the challenges of Christian faith but instead to admit how deep they are and how much still needs to change in us as we seek to follow Christ.

2. It's really important to remember the difference between 'Religion' and 'faith' here. As I said in Chapter 1, 'Religion' is the systematic organization and practices around a certain Faith whereas 'faith' is the act of believing. We must also remember that those who claim affiliation to a Religion may not necessarily have faith in its founder in the way I am suggesting. Hence those who claim to be Muslims but act aggressively, for example, are not actually Muslims in the truest sense of the word. In the same way those who claim to be members of the Christian Religion may not necessarily have faith in or be followers of Jesus Christ.

## Look at Jesus – did he make sense?

If God exists, and if he has demonstrated himself uniquely in his son Jesus, then taking Jesus seriously must be one of the greatest needs of our time. The Jesus of the New Testament was a radical figure. His words rocked the religious establishment and challenged the *status quo*. For those today who seek to take him seriously, Jesus' example and teaching are a call to radical transformation – of ourselves and then of the communities of which we are part and the worlds in which we live.

There are a number of deep challenges that the life and teaching of Jesus presents us with. The deepest of them is that he claimed to be both God and man. The absolutely unique claim of Christian faith is that in Jesus both humanity and divinity lived together. C.S. Lewis was right:

> that people often say about Him: 'I'm ready to accept Jesus as a great moral teacher, but I don't accept His claim to be God.' That is the one thing we must not say. A man who was merely a man and said the sort of things Jesus said would not be a great moral teacher. He would either be a lunatic – on a level with the man who says he is a poached egg – or else he would be the Devil of Hell. You must make your choice. Either this man was, and is, the Son of God: or else a madman or something worse. You can shut Him up for a fool, you can spit at Him and kill Him as a demon; or you can fall at His feet and call Him Lord and God. But let us not come with any patronising nonsense about His being a great human teacher. He has not left that open to us. He did not intend to.[3]

Jesus Christ was deeply motivated to overcome exclusion and to bring forgiveness, acceptance and justice to the world. It is precisely *because* of his humanity and his divinity that this commitment is so challenging. As a human being he shows us that a better world can be built. He demonstrates that human beings can live in community well. He demonstrates that compassion and love and

3. C.S. Lewis, *Mere Christianity* (1898–1963).

fairness and dignity are all traits of character that we fellow human beings can display. As God, Jesus also shows us that we are tremendously valuable to God and that we are each viewed as significant. God is so committed to us that he lives amongst us and demonstrates ways in which we can relate to one another as well as we relate to him.

Taking the teaching of the New Testament seriously is a dangerous affair. In fact, the Jesus of the New Testament was so radical compared to much of what was widely understood as Christianity in the 19th century that the American author Mark Twain once commented that if Jesus was alive in Twain's day the one thing Christ would not be is a Christian! It is challenging to consider whether the same could be said today. Millions of people around the world are followers of Christ – they have examined his teachings and seek to take him seriously. However, we are none of us perfect, and so those who seek to follow Jesus are still flawed followers. While this is a challenge that Christians should be reminded of, it should not be a stick with which to beat the one we follow! Although I am a Christ-follower, my personal failings do not change the authenticity of Jesus. For those who aspire to make a difference in the world, there is no better example than Jesus.

In his own declaration of intent in Nazareth he announced a very radical manifesto:

> The Spirit of the Lord is on me
> Because he has anointed me
> To preach good news to the poor.
> He has sent me to proclaim freedom for the prisoners
> And recovery of sight for the blind,
> To release the oppressed,
> To proclaim the year of the Lord's favour.[4]

This is a manifesto of radical change. At the heart of Christian faith lies a commitment by Jesus to connect with and serve the poor, the oppressed and the excluded, as we saw in our examination of the

4. Luke 4.18ff; Isaiah 61.1ff.

beatitudes. Too often, the example of Jesus has been over-spiritualized. Perhaps because his words and actions are so deeply challenging, his intentions have been translated into solely spiritual ones. To turn Jesus into a figure of history with a 'spiritual message' that is somehow disconnected with the reality of life is a gross misrepresentation. His words and his actions clearly matched. In first-century Palestine new religious teachers were a dime a dozen. Yet Jesus' impact continues today. Why is that? The Jews in Palestine were creaking under the weight of religious expectation from a legalistic system that had prescribed almost everything that they could or could not do. Not only that, they were living under Roman occupation, enduring a foreign power's exploitation. For the poor and the marginalized in this cauldron of religious and political oppression, Jesus' words and example gave hope. His promise to help the poor, to stand with the excluded and to set prisoners free spoke to the heart of their pain and frustration. He did not come with lengthy expectations and demands that needed to be met before he helped. He came to help, to serve and to love. He came to make a practical difference and a spiritual difference in the lives of others. But he did both *at the same time*. Of course he called for *followers* not just *hearers*. But he provided acceptance and love *before* allegiance was given, not after it. People knew he cared.

The ultimate demonstration of his commitment and his life is found in his willingness to sacrifice himself for others. The cross may be a potent symbol of pain and loss, but it is also a powerful symbol of hope. It must always be viewed within the context of the *whole* life and ministry of Jesus Christ, but it must never be forgotten. It is a stake in the ground. It lifts the life and example and commitment of Jesus way above anything and anyone else. In it he ultimately defeats the powers that make the world such a difficult and painful place. In the cross is found the key to personal transformation and the transformation of the world. Somehow, mysteriously, in the cross we see all of God's power and all of God's strength demonstrated. As Jesus suffers and dies, those who suffer find someone they can relate to. Those who sacrifice find the ultimate example. Those who need forgiveness find the ultimate replacement and sacrifice. The cross may be painful to consider but it is unavoidable. It speaks of commitment, love, endurance and a willingness to take the place of another. It is the key that unlocks the chains that bind millions of people around the world. It is inexplicable in its power to transform because Jesus did this *for me* and *for you*. This is not some kind of non-personal act. The mystery is this: the cross changes not only the individual who embraces it but also the whole world.

We must also remember the resurrection – the ultimate symbol of hope and joy. Following from the pain of the cross which is the Divine 'no' to the pain and suffering and evil in the world, those of Christian faith believe that the resurrection is the Divine 'yes' to change and transformation. Jesus rising again reminds those who have Christian faith that ultimately the world *will be transformed*. There is always hope.

It is impossible to look at the Jesus of the New Testament and not be challenged. If we are really going to take Jesus seriously, how can we personally apply his example and teachings to our own attitudes, behaviour and life choices?

## Challenge 1: Treating people with dignity

While I was leading a church in the South of England a couple in the congregation had a baby. Delighted at the birth of their daughter, they gave her the name Hope. As time progressed it became clear that there was something unusual about Hope's development. After a vast array of tests and countless visits to the hospital, she was diagnosed as having a very rare medical condition. She would never develop physiologically or intellectually beyond the age of two or three. She would be blind and deaf and unable to speak. Yet her parents, not unexpectedly, continued to love and cherish this little girl. Their bravery, stamina and commitment were breathtaking examples of love. They asked me to dedicate Hope – to publicly thank God for her and commit her future to his keeping. I counted this a privilege and was happy to agree to the request. On the morning of her dedication, I preached from a simple text found in the Old Testament:

And God said let us make humankind in our image. In the image of God he made them; male and female he created them.[5]

Hope may not be able to speak, to see or hear, but because she is a human being, she demands my respect and the respect of every other person. She does not need to earn dignity – she has dignity because God has made her. The same is true of all people.

Hope's story challenges us because it is so straightforward. This little girl will never be able to relate to me. She will never be able to have a conversation with me. She will never be 'like other people'. Yet she is equal in God's sight to me, you and to every other person. Her worth does not come from her ability, her intellect or her faith. As we saw in Chapter 3, her worth and dignity flow from the fact that she is made by God. There are people in all of our communities who are different from us. Their difference might flow from their abilities, their colour or their preferences. They may be different, but they are no less valuable than us. They are entitled to and deserve our respect as much as anyone else.

Jesus treats all people with dignity. Remembering the close relationship between Christian faith and Jewish faith and the fact that Jesus was a Jew helps us to understand why. Embedded deeply within the Jewish understanding of life is the belief that every human being is made in God's image.[6] There are a variety of ways in which this concept has been interpreted philosophically and theologically through the centuries. Most of the discussion has revolved around the *idea* or *concept* of what it means to be made in the image of God. These arguments have rarely resulted in a discussion about the *relational* implications of every human being bearing God's image.[7] Yet, the practical implications of what it means to be made in the image of God must be taken seriously if we are to take Jesus seriously. A spirituality that does not treat people with dignity cannot claim to be a Christian spirituality. Put

---

5. These words are found right at the beginning of the Bible in Genesis 1.27.
6. Genesis 1.27; Psalm 139.13ff.
7. For those interested in exploring those arguments, see Anthony A. Hoekema, *Created in God's Image* (Grand Rapids: Eerdmans, 1986), particularly chapter 5 *The Image of God: A Theological Summary*.

simply, the example of Jesus tells me that there are no human beings less important to God than I am.

An Iraqi, an African, an Arab and an American are equal. A Catholic, a Protestant, a Jew, a Hindu or a Sikh are all made in God's image. The married couple, the gay man, the lesbian and the transsexual – all are worthy of our respect, our time and our unconditional love and service. 'Disability' is not part of God's vocabulary. There are no examples of Jesus refusing help to people in the New Testament. He did not 'means test' those who came to him. He did not turn them away. He helped them. The challenge of taking him seriously is that we must do the same.

If there was no one whom Jesus did not respect and help, and if we are going to be serious about following his example, then there is no one whom we should not respect and help. I would go further. Our shared humanity and our shared sense of being bearers of God's image connects us more deeply than we realize. The ache that we feel when we see a child die needlessly from a lack of clean water is precisely because both that child and we are made in the image of the same God. The motivation to buy a Make Poverty History armband and campaign for the cancellation of world debt springs from the reality of our deep connectedness with other human beings. Wherever there is a commitment to the dignity of life and people, that commitment springs from the spiritual connection shared by all people: we all share the same source of life. In that sense the Christian God is the universal God – the God of the whole earth.[8] It is a bold and an audacious claim, but it is not made less true because of its boldness or its audacity. The Christian view of the dignity of all life is one of the most important principles for transforming any society imaginable. It also demands a response. If we recognize God in one another, we will never be the same again.

8. The Roman Catholic theologian Karl Rahner coined the phrase 'anonymous Christian' in his writing to suggest that it was possible for people to be followers of Christ without realizing it. His argument was largely theoretical, but I am suggesting that there is a pragmatic sense in which all good actions, all good deeds and all goodness itself finds its source in God. If you are interested in reading more of Rahner's ideas, then *Theological Investigations* (London: Darton, Longman and Todd, 1966) is a good place to start. Particularly pp. 115–34 of vol. V.

How I treat my neighbours will display whether or not I have grasped this principle. Often we treat people differently because we do not understand them. That lack of understanding leads us to make judgements that may be superficial or even false. While most of us would not consider ourselves 'prejudiced' there are occasions in our lives and in our judgements when we jump to a wrong conclusion because of a lack of understanding on our part of another person's difference or distinctiveness. When we do not understand someone, we tend to fear them — and when we fear someone we either avoid them or attack and criticize them. Furthermore, how I treat those who personify my deepest fears and uncertainties shows whether or not I am a true follower of Christ. Too often our opinions are formed by our fears and lack of understanding and therefore our relationships and commitments are formed by the same things. If we struggle with understanding sexuality, for example, then we might treat gay people as less than equal to ourselves. If we struggle with race and ethnicity then we might treat people of a different colour or background as having less value than ourselves. Such views are exposed and challenged by the example of Christ. We will never build a better world if we demand the right to hold on to our views and opinions if those views and opinions are shaped by fear and lack of understanding.

## Challenge 2: Recognizing that life is holistic

When we take Jesus seriously we discover a figure who powerfully shakes our *status quo* and calls us to leave our comfort zones. For Jesus, the physical life and the non-physical life were deeply connected. For him, all of life was important. A cup of cold water given to someone in his name had both pragmatic and spiritual consequences. He washed people's feet — even the feet of those who would become his enemies, demonstrating grace and commitment even to those who would hurt him. For the Jesus of the New Testament, all of life was sacred.

Jesus did not live in a secular and sacred divide. Every space for him was a holy space. Every action was a spiritual action — or an action that is connected both to what we see and what we can't see. For him all people were spiritual. The Jesus of the New Testament earthed spirituality in life and celebrated life as spiritual. His words were demonstrated by his actions and his actions were explained in his words. His manifesto was not just a list of poetic images tied to spiritual emancipation. This carpenter from Nazareth came to actually set people free, to feed the hungry, to release prisoners and to serve and empower the excluded. He recognized that physical needs and social change were important. He was an ordinary radical. Yet he lived out the principle that you cannot see social change in isolation from spiritual and emotional change.

The challenge of this integral life is profound. For most people in the West, our views of Jesus have been formed by our encounters with the institutionalized Church. That is perhaps why many people are inspired by Jesus, but often put off by the Church! Consider this quote from Bono:

> Everywhere I look I see the evidence of a Creator. But I don't see it as religion, which has cut my people in two. I don't see Jesus Christ as being part of a religion. Religion to me is almost like when God leaves – and people devise a set of rules to fill the space.[9]

In Jim Wallis's book, *God's Politics*, he articulates this dichotomy of understanding by asking questions like 'When did Jesus become pro-rich, pro-American or pro-war?'[10] Somehow, Jesus and the Church have become disconnected. Yet, Jesus is our prime example and he is the head of the Church! The example of Christ upsets our assumptions and overturns our misconceptions precisely because we have allowed our assumptions to be built around a wrong understanding of God and of his Son. Perhaps we need to get to know the Jesus who walks the pages of the New Testament rather than the Jesus who stalks the aisles of many churches? The

9. Bono, quoted in Steven Stockman, *Walk On: The Spiritual Journey of U2* (Orlando: Relevant Media Group Inc., 2005).
10. See Jim Wallis's *God's Politics*.

real Jesus, the forgotten Jesus, may be very different from the one we thought existed. The challenge each of us faces in taking Jesus seriously is not only in studying his actions and words – it is also in emulating them. There is also a challenge for us in recognizing the deep connection between spirituality and social change. Since 1945 and the establishment of the welfare state in the United Kingdom, successive governments have invested billions of pounds in protecting the vulnerable and the poor in Britain. Yet the past decade has seen a growing realization that government programmes and investment will not solve the problems of exclusion and poverty. Sociologically any change that is forced upon us will not last very long. As we have seen, for meaningful and sustainable change to take place it must be a change that we *choose* to participate in. The only people who can change a community are those who are part of that community. And they can only change that community if they themselves change. Transformation cannot be done 'to' anyone – it must be chosen by each of us. Transformation of our street, our community and our society cannot take place without inner change. True change flows from within to without.

Take the example of disaffected young people who are excluded from school because of unruly behaviour and reactions against authority. The Lighthouse Group, a Christian educational trust in Bradford in the UK, works with such excluded young people. Lighthouse recognizes that in order to change the educational achievement of these young people it must start with how the young people feel about themselves. For that reason, Lighthouse spends a great deal of time helping young people to understand what they want to achieve out of life. Through mentoring programmes, listening, befriending and detached support and guidance, Lighthouse encourages the young people it works with to face the causes of their behaviour and deal with those. An intrinsic part of its support and help is enabling young people to explore their own spirituality and their lives in a joined-up way. The charity sees some amazing results. Young people who have been told that they are beyond help are turned around because they are helped to confront the issues in their own lives.

Prison Fellowship is another example of change flowing from

within. Founded by Charles Colson, the charity works with people in prison and helps them to explore their own spirituality. Again and again prisoners report a complete change in their attitudes and behaviour as a result of discovering the spiritual side of their lives and pursuing a relationship with God. This spiritual change leads to a transformed life as ex-offenders move forward with a different set of values and commitments. Their external lives are transformed through a clearer, more focused spirituality.

Spiritual and social change are two sides of the same coin. We lose one at the expense of the other. To deny our own spirituality or the spirituality of others is to deny the very seedbed of transformation and hope from which lasting change can grow.

## Challenge 3: Becoming the change we want to see

There is nothing worse than hearing someone tell you how everything should be when you know that they are not living out what they are saying; we either see such people as 'full of hot air' or view them as hypocritical and judgemental. We instinctively withdraw from them. In the words of Gandhi we must become the change that we want to see.

Jesus did not only talk about spending time with the marginalized and vulnerable, he touched lepers, had dinner with tax collectors and honoured and respected women. He could have just talked about feeding hungry people but instead he fed them. He could have talked about caring for the sick but instead he made them well. He could have just talked about religious hypocrisy and exploitation, but instead he drove tax collectors from the temple in Jerusalem.

There are shining examples of inspirational practitioners who have taken the teaching and example of Jesus seriously and sought to emulate it. Bob Holman is one such example. Bob was a social worker and academic in Bath but left his career to go and live with the people of Easterhouse in Scotland. He did not believe that he could speak about the poor, or that he could speak on behalf of the poor. Instead he is convinced that the poor should tell their own story. He also knows that his own words and actions lack sincerity and depth unless they are backed by action and commitment. A committed Christian, Bob believes that followers of Christ must live out the message and the commandments of Christ. He is seeking to do that still. The result has been that many people in Easterhouse have been able to tell their own stories to those in power, both in Scotland and in Westminster. Not only that, people on the Easterhouse estate who know Bob know that they have someone who believes in them and treats them as equals. They see in Bob someone who shares his life, not just his faith. This commitment and vulnerability has meant that people have trusted Bob. Their defences have gone down as they have witnessed his whole-hearted sharing of his life. This has resulted in people finding a way out of hopelessness and despair. Some have been helped out of debt, some out of abusive relationships. Others have simply found that they can make something of their lives and have discovered a whole new future. Because they have been told a different story about themselves their lives have been changed for the better. If we want our communities to be safer places, then perhaps we must contribute to crime reduction and crime prevention ourselves by starting a neighbourhood watch or keeping an eye on the house next door? If we want to see poverty eradicated, then perhaps we must learn to shop differently, bank differently and vote differently?

We must also remember that if we are to become the change that we ultimately want to see, it will cost us. Jackie Pullinger left the United Kingdom in order to live in the walled city of Hong Kong. She went with no money, no support and no organization behind her. Yet she lived amongst the men and women of the walled city. She served, loved and wept with those who were addicted to drugs or whose lives had been torn apart by violence. Her motivation was to see the people with whom she worked set free from powerful addictions and released to be all that they could be. She gave up everything to live amongst the people of the walled city. Yet she would say that she gained a great deal as well. The fact remains, however, that if we are to see lasting change in the lives of people we seek to serve, there is often a deep cost to us personally. What Bob Holman and Jackie Pullinger have in common is that they were both willing to pay the price exacted upon them in order to see the change that they longed for.

The Faithworks Movement is made up of people who have sacrificed heavily in order to see change in their communities. They have given up lucrative salaries, comfortable homes and respectable positions in society in order to see their communities changed and the disadvantaged helped. For these modern-day heroes, the sacrifice is worth it because people matter.

## Challenge 4: Taking Church seriously[11]

Jesus' radicalism not only challenges our society, it challenges his followers and therefore it challenges his Church:

> I'm not so comfortable in the Church, it feels so pious and so unlike the Christ that I read about in the scriptures.[12]

I've already suggested that there are many people who respect Jesus and agree with his teaching, but are put off by the Church. Yet as flawed as the Church is, she is still a beautiful bride in the eyes of God. With all of its faults and failings, the Church is still making a lasting difference in communities across the world. Whether or not we *attend* a church, when we are following Christ, we are part of God's family on earth.

Perhaps if we can begin to understand Church differently it will help. The Church is not a structure. The Church is a set of relationships with Jesus at the centre. At any given point those who are part of the Church – those who are somehow following Christ, can be closer to him or further from him. We are part of the Church when we are close to Christ and we are part of the Church when we are far from him. In other words, the only people who

---

11. I have included a postscript at the end of this book addressed directly to those who consider themselves to be followers of Christ already and count themselves as part of the Church. It's a plea from a fellow traveller.
12. Bono, quoted in Cathleen Falsani, 'Bono's American Prayer', *Christianity Today* 47, no. 3 (2003).

are not part of the Church are those who deliberately choose not to be. Across the United Kingdom and the US there are a growing number of vibrant Christian communities that are exploring what this means. John Burke began a Christian community now known as Gateway Community Church in Austin, Texas which now has over two thousand members. It is a church family where people are welcomed as they are. In Bournemouth in Dorset, Rob Clark leads a Christian community called 'Bournemouth Vineyard'. The strapline of the church is, 'Where the imperfect are perfectly welcome'. In London Christian communities meet in pubs, clubs and sports centres. Church.co.uk/waterloo, led by Dave Steell, is found in the London borough of Lambeth, within a stone's throw of Westminster. Dave's vision is to see the Christian community there serving those who live in the area twenty-four hours a day seven days a week. At the time of writing, the church community provide in excess of 120 hours of service and care. They will soon be open round the clock. Cedar Ridge Community Church in Spencerville, Maryland, led by Brian McLaren, is another example of a community of faith which is open at the edges and welcoming people who want to explore their faith and spirituality. All of these Christian communities, together with thousands of others, are taking Jesus very seriously and hundreds of thousands of people are living out radical lifestyles as they follow him. They invite and enable people to belong to their community before they believe. They refuse to be judgemental. These groups meet in houses, hotels, pubs and traditional church buildings. They have varied styles, formats and ideas. They are not seeking to do anything more than follow in the footsteps of Jesus. They are part of a silent but powerful revolution in thinking and practice across the world. They share two common bonds – they take Jesus and each other very seriously indeed. Having said that, can we perhaps challenge the priorities of the Church? The great 19th-century reformer, Charles Finney, said this:

> The Great Business of the Church is to reform the world . . . the church of Christ was originally formed to be a body of re-formers. The very profession of Christianity implies the

profession and virtually an oath to do all that can be done for the universal reformation of the world.[13]

The Church does not exist for its own benefit. Being a follower of Christ demands that we become servants of others – and that we serve together. The true and genuine responsibility of the Church is to be an agent of hope and transformation in the world. This can only happen as ordinary men and women take up their place within the Church to effect change within society.

One of the hallmarks of Jesus' teaching was that it was very straightforward. He did not use confusing and complicated concepts and ideas. He used the language of the everyday to help people understand life and its deep connectedness to God. So he used images like salt and light and yeast in his conversations with people to help them see that their lives could make a difference.[14] These images highlight the fact that a little contribution can make a big difference. A little light dispels a great deal of darkness. A little salt enhances flavour greatly. A little yeast will cause bread to rise. The three images also show that too much of them, or an inappropriate use of them, can do harm. Too much light blinds, too much salt destroys flavour and too much yeast causes bread to become all air and no substance. There is a lesson for us all here. As small and insignificant as we may feel, we each have a pivotal part to play in the transformation of our communities and our society. We should not force change, we should not even force our own faith. Instead, we do what we can, when we can. We grow in faith and trust naturally, not unnaturally.

Within walking distance of most urban church buildings in the United Kingdom, 10,000 people live. These people each face their own struggles and challenges. They are not just statistics. Each person has a name, a family, a history. They are people who have longings and dreams as well as heartbreaks and disappointments. The challenges that they face are great. This 'typical' community would look something like this:[15]

13. Charles G. Finney, *Lectures on Revival* (Minneapolis: Bethany House Publishers, 1988), chapter 1: *What is Revival?*
14. Matthew 5 and 13.
15. Tim Chester, *Good News to the Poor: The Gospel and Social Action* (Leicester: IVP, 2003).

- 1,200 people living alone, of whom 580 will be of pensionable age
- 1,500 people who talk to their neighbours less than once a week
- 50 people who have been divorced in the last year
- 375 people who are single parents
- 18 teenage girls who are pregnant
- 150 women who have contemplated or had an abortion recently
- 250 people who are unemployed
- 1,700 people living in a low-income household
- 1,100 people living with mental illness
- 100 people who were bereaved in the last year
- 2,700 people with no car
- 60 people who live in residential care
- 1,280 people caring for a sick, elderly or disabled friend or relative
- 2,800 people who have been victims of crime
- 40 people who are homeless or living in temporary accommodation
- 15 people who are asylum seekers.

Across the United Kingdom, local churches are working together to make a difference in many of these people's lives. They do so not looking for recognition and applause, but because they genuinely care about the people in their community. The participants in those local Christian faith communities serve in parent and toddler groups. Their buildings are used for self-help groups. They seek to work alongside those in the community. Followers of Christ are listening and working with others to transform communities. They do not believe that they alone can turn communities around. Instead they are working in partnership with voluntary groups, statutory and government groups and other faith communities to make a difference. For those who serve Christ, every person matters – every one has a name. The numbers we have just read are not just statistics. They are neighbours and family members.

It is these people that the Church is supposed to engage with. As individual followers of Jesus and as communities of faith, we have a responsibility to those who consider themselves to be hopeless, helpless or forgotten. The Church in the United Kingdom employs more youth workers than any other voluntary body. The Church is the only movement in the UK that has a presence in every single community across the country. More people attend church than go to football matches across the leagues in the United Kingdom. So far from being a monolithic, unchangeable and irrelevant body, the Church in the United Kingdom is helping to build a better world for millions of people.

Whether we are beginning the journey of faith or well along the path, there are common values that we can hold which will bind us together rather than pull us apart. Perhaps by joining forces with other people who share our commitments, our ideals and even a growing faith, we can make an even greater impact on our world. One simple step might be to consider becoming part of a local church. Although the idea might seem strange at first, it might just be possible that a community of fellow travellers will energize, encourage and support us as we try to connect our spirituality with our commitments to justice, compassion and the eradication of poverty. It might be frustrating, but it might also provide a safe haven. A local Christian community provides us with a place of safety for exploration, contemplation and company. It offers us a group of people with whom we can build a relationship and explore spirituality from within a Christian context. It connects us to thousands of years of history, yet feeds our search for a spiritual anchor point and a purpose to our lives. And it works.

## Religion or relationship?

The faith in Christ that I have is what gives me strength to carry on. My spirituality is what enables me to make a contribution to my community and my town. When I engage with other people I bring my convictions and ideas, but I also bring my relationship with God. While I refuse to force my faith upon others or demand that they believe, in being part of a community I bring my own ongoing encounter with God with me. I cannot divorce my convictions from my actions, nor would I want to. Instead, I seek to model an understanding of God and of Truth that others are free to explore with me. I cannot unpack my Christian convictions about God in three simple sound-bites and a four-point plan. I do not fully understand God and have a great deal to learn. I am, however, certain that God is Truth. By being in relationship with God, I am in relationship with Truth. This is the difference between relationship and religion.

My conviction is that some have been trying to 'teach' or 'impose' the truth for too long. People cannot be forced to believe anything – this too often has been the purpose of 'religion'. The purpose of life, the reason for existence and the ways in which we can build a better world cannot be written in a short essay or book and learned and then forced upon other people. These are questions whose answers unfold as our lives unfold. They are questions that push us forward in life, that cause us to change and develop and grow. Such questions make us better people as we probe them. As we improve our understanding of ourselves, others and our place in the world, we help build a better world both physically and spiritually. For the follower of Christ, truth cannot be summarized in a statement. Some short statements, like 'murder is wrong' or 'treating people justly is right' can be truthful and can fully describe a belief or conviction but this is not the same as condensing the whole of truth down in to a single statement. Deeper truth cannot just be written down. There is a simple reason for that. My Christian faith has taught me that the Truth is a person – and his name is Jesus.[16] If the Truth is a person, then the way we relate to him is entirely different to the way in which we relate to a statement.

I can 'know' and 'learn' a statement fully. I can recite it word for word. I can never fully know a person. I know them in a growing, changing and evolving way. My relationships with my family members are an example. I have four children – two boys and two girls. I know 'facts' about them – but that is not the same as knowing them. I can tell you the colour of their eyes, their hair,

---

16. To read more about what this means from the point of view of the New Testament and the early followers of Christ, John's Gospel, particularly chapters 14–17, where Jesus' conversations with his followers immediately prior to his death are recorded.

the schools they go to, their favourite colours and what they enjoy doing. But that does not mean I 'know' them completely. My wife and I are the two closest people to our children in the world, yet we are constantly amazed at how much more there is to know about them. Our knowledge of the facts that describe them does not encompass the fuller way of knowing *them*.

The same is true with the Truth. We can learn aspects of the truth through our lives that can be summarized as statements. Poverty is wrong and should stop. Human trafficking is a disgrace. Unfair trade agreements are destroying lives. There are too many poor children in America and the United Kingdom, and elsewhere in the world. Racism is a blight upon our societies. These are all true statements. Yet if these statements are anchored in a relationship with the Truth, they become part of an understanding of the world that is joined up, that has cohesion. They are not *diminished* by such association, they are *enhanced*. Poverty is wrong *because* God shows us the dignity of all human life as we walk with Christ – and the more we walk with him the more we understand poverty and how deeply it is wrong. The statement that poverty is wrong springs from our understanding of life and the world as we glimpse it in our developing relationship with God, through Christ. As we get to know him, as we take him seriously, as we walk with him and learn from him, we *learn* the Truth as a companion learns about another, not just as a reader learns from a textbook. This then leads to spirituality that is open, growing, developing and evolving. Faith becomes a journey rather than a destination. Christian faith connects to a spirituality that offers us the chance to explore Truth as a lifelong pilgrimage. It opens us up to the chance not only to learn from God through Christ, but to learn from one another. In fact, we can learn from every person for precisely the same reason as we care about other people. They, too, are made in God's image and we can meet God in them. Even if they do not believe in God, God believes in them.

Christian faith leads to a spirituality that offers a view of life and the world that treats others as equals whether they share Christian faith or not. It is a spirituality that addresses the inequalities of the world. It recognizes that the line between good and bad passes not through nations, but through every human heart. It recognizes that we are part of the problem as well as the solution and that in order to build a better world we must also address the issues in our own lives and hearts that need attention. It offers a brighter view of the future and the possibility of genuine change and transformation. It closes the imaginary gap between the physical and the spiritual and helps to join up responses to human need. It points to a connection between people and God, between the earth and its maker, between the inner longing for change that every person experiences and the One who can bring true change to all who seek it.

The challenge for us is to become individuals who are truly guided by the example and life of Christ in all that we say and do. Christian faith might just enable us to be in relationship with the Truth rather than learn it off by heart. Such relationship might avoid the pitfalls of Religion in order to embrace genuine spirituality.

We began this chapter asking how we can take all that we have discussed personally. To answer that question, those of us who have a deep passion for justice, and desire to explore that holistically, need to take seriously the role of faith in our own lives as well as those we seek to serve. As we allow faith to grow and develop in our own lives, we will grow to realize that change must be spiritual as well as physical. In fact changing how we understand ourselves is a prerequisite to how we change our world. For that reason, Christian faith not only matters, it matters to me and to you individually. Taking Christian faith seriously at a personal level means we begin to explore our own relationship with God and with others who are on a similar journey. We begin to see ourselves as part of a community of fellow travellers. None of us is perfect, but each of us has a part to play. We recognize that each of us has imperfections, failings and faulty understanding but that somehow we need each other if we are to build a better world. That leaves us with a nagging question which acts like a continually dripping tap in our heads and our hearts – where do we go from here? Until we attempt to answer that question, the tap will continue to drip.

# Moving on 6

*Where do we go from here?*

Without a biblical worldview, all the great teaching goes in one ear and out the other. There are no intellectual pegs ... in the mind of the individual to hang these truths on. So they just pass through. They don't stick. They don't make a difference.[1]

To stay quiet is as political an act as speaking out.[2]

What do we do with all of this 'stuff'? The principles, the charter and the challenges are all well and good, but what difference does it make to our lives on a day-to-day basis? What do we do in response to the example and teaching of Christ? Clearly, if we read this book and *nothing* changes then the book itself will have achieved little and we may well have wasted some precious time. In this chapter, I want to suggest ways forward that we might want to explore.

## Recap

To start with, let me take us back to two questions I asked right back in Chapter 1:

What if your passion for change in the world was given to you by God? What if Christian faith works?

1. George Barna, as quoted in Charles Colson and Nancy Pearson, *How Now Shall We Live* (London: HarperCollins, 1999), Introduction, p. ix.
2. Arundhati Roy, author and Indian activist.

I've tried to articulate my convictions about the connection between Christian faith and making the world a better place. In Chapter 1, I made the point that I think there is a viable and important place in the world for faith in the 21st century. In Chapter 2, I suggested that faith may be a personal choice but that it has consequences on the entire way that we live and the way we relate to others. Chapter 3 unpacked the impact of part of Jesus' teaching in the Sermon on the Mount and helped us to reset our compass. In Chapter 4 we went further and asserted ten positive principles that Christian faith contributes to a healthy and strong society. In Chapter 5 we explored that holding a view doesn't change anything except our mind, but that living according to that view changes everything. Edmund Burke said that evil prospers when good people do nothing. The choice that you as a reader and I as an author must make is what we will *do* in the light of what we know.

## 1. Recognize that change is possible

It is easy to look at the world and believe that change is not possible – that we are somehow fighting a battle that cannot be won. On 1 May 2006, more than 1 million people took to the streets of the United States in one of the biggest protests in American history. From New York to Los Angeles, more than fifty cities were flooded with migrant workers who were protesting against proposed new immigration laws. The protests are being dubbed 'The Great American Boycott'. The predominantly Latino protesters were determined to make their voice heard – and it worked. Around 300,000 people protested in Los Angeles, 400,000 people took to the streets of Chicago. The crowds were made up of immigrants' rights groups, undocumented and documented 'migrants' and schoolchildren. Blowing whistles and banging drums, they wanted to know why they were good enough to work in the US but not good enough to have residency rights. As the protesters surged through cities, they were chanting a song – 'Si, se puede'. Translated it means 'Yes, it can be done'. It remains to be seen whether the demonstrations will prove successful. Those involved have certainly shown that there is a Latino political lobby in the US that can no longer be ignored. Their chant caught my imagination, though. I think those of us who long for justice and an eradication of poverty face a huge challenge. The obstacles are great, the opposition huge, but perhaps we ourselves must learn to sing, like the protesters on the streets of the US, 'Si, se puede', 'Yes, it can be done'.

We need to be open to seeing God at work in the world *through us* and others. In the hands and feet and words and actions of other people, will we begin to see God at work? Are we able to see that behind their acts of kindness, their compassionate responses and their commitment to doing something about the problems of the world there may well be One Source of love, grace and goodness? Indeed, are we willing to consider the possibility that behind *our* acts of kindness, compassionate responses and commitments to do something about the problems of the world the same One Source of love, grace and goodness has been at work?

It is entirely possible that we are instruments of God already; it is just that we have not been aware of it until now. What we thought was an inconsequential act was actually a life-changing one inhabited by God's presence and love. In that sense, we may be a channel of God's power to change the world without even knowing that God is at work through us. In fact, I don't think it is just a possibility; I think it is the truth. We have been the change that we want to see, and God has been silently and powerfully working through us and in our own lives. He has been waiting for us to see him, but he has not taken his eyes off us for a single second.

The decision to see God at work through our acts and those of others suddenly changes everything. We are no longer fighting a tide that cannot be defeated. Instead we are working with the tide. We are moving in the right direction, not the wrong one. We no longer see our own life and commitments in quite the same way as we did before. Our acts of kindness become part of a tapestry of compassion that is enfolding the earth. Our strand retains its colour, its vibrancy, its texture and its beauty but it now complements the threads of others and is complemented by them. In recognizing the other threads, our work and commitments are not diminished in any way; instead they are enhanced – made *more* beautiful, *more* meaningful, *more* needed.

## 2. Explore our spirituality, don't hide from it

For those who began this book wondering what role Christian faith had to play in their lives, there are just as many issues to consider, but perhaps they are slightly different. I am convinced that the desire, conviction and longing to build a better world all have strong connections with Christian faith and spirituality. Each of us must explore that for ourselves, and that exploration will continue long after the reading of this book has finished. Indeed, the reading of these words might just be the start of the journey.

In the midst of a society that has grown to see Christian faith as something of an anachronism we have the task of showing that Christian faith and spirituality have as much to say today as they have ever done. We need to allow our inner spirituality to spill into the society of which we are part. Instead of seeking to convert the world, we want to converse with those around us. Such a journey is demanding but rewarding. It demands some pretty significant changes in the way we 'do' things, but many followers of Christ have realized that. Across the United Kingdom and the United States there are wonderfully exciting expressions of Christian spirituality and holistic mission springing up. There are many Christian communities that welcome those who want to explore their spirituality.

From Fairtrade Café in Yorkshire and Humber, which is a fresh and exciting expression of Christian faith built around ethical trading, to Urban Expressions, an innovative inner-city approach to Christian community, the UK is seeing more and more innovative and creative communities that are seeking to express their faith through all of their lives, not just when they meet together. The growth and expansion of the cell church model also mirrors this emerging trend toward whole life engagement. The development and growth of churches in the US such as Willow Creek community church in Chicago and Rick Warren's Saddle-back Community Church in Orange County, California also show that churches in America are developing creative models of expression that allow for diversity and difference and focus on the whole of life. Willow Creek and Saddleback are not developing 'production line' followers of Christ. Instead these mega-churches are succeeding in developing disciples of Christ that are engaged, committed and determined to make their faith relevant to all of their lives.

Yet at the same time, across the West there are small expressions of Christian community springing up. They are finding one another in chat rooms and blogs, exploring fellowship and mutual support through conversation and letter writing. These are organic communities committed to modelling Christ. Bliss is an emerging church in Dorset in the UK which is committed to mentoring, relationships and one-to-one support. It's another example of a very different approach to Christian community. The average size of a church congregation in the UK is just 47, and in the US it is under 100.

These are delicate flowers in one sense, apparently vulnerable to criticism, attack and the possibility of withering as quickly as they have grown. Yet my feeling is that these 'delicate flowers' have strong and deep roots. The leaders of emerging Christian communities that I have spoken to often find themselves criticized by the more traditional churches. They can be seen as 'lightweight' in terms of commitment and 'theology'. One leader of an emerging church that I spoke to recently told me of his frustrations at being seen as 'on the edge' of the Church. Yet the truth is that the roots of emerging churches are just as deep as those of other Christian communities that have bought into intellectualism and an enlightenment approach to Truth.

The reverse can also be true, with emerging churches overly criticizing traditional and established congregations for their lack of connectedness. Traditional churches often feel that the inherent attitude of new and emerging Christian communities is one of cynicism. In the town where I live there have been real efforts to build unity across the different expressions of church by focusing on the purpose of engagement with the community – and it is working, with new partnerships being forged and new ideas being shared.[3] Those who are followers of Christ may be living in days that are wonderfully inspiring, challenging and rewarding. We can care for the delicate flowers of new Christian community while at the same time tending and pruning those that are more traditional. We might be a generation of followers of Christ that become a bridge between what has been and what is to be. Such a responsibility demands humility, sensitivity and commitment, but something tells me that many of the followers of Jesus that I have met hold those qualities in great measure. Fellow travellers must learn from each other.

## 3. Move beyond debate[4]

We need to decide whether we have a debate about Christian faith or begin a conversation with God? The difference is profound. A debate can be carried on in the third person; it is an intellectual interchange of ideas and perspectives. A conversation is personal. One of the basic commitments I made right at the beginning of *Building a Better World* was that I would not seek to 'convert' through what I was trying to articulate. I am determined to remain true to that commitment. The decision that you as a reader must now make is whether you believe that it is possible to begin a conversation with God or not. That might be as simple a step as asking 'Are you there?'

It might be that the conversation begins around the particular area of work we are involved in or the challenges we face at this moment in our lives. *Why is this happening to my community? How do*

---

3. I live in Reading in Berkshire, and through the work of groups like the Reading Christian Network and Impact Reading, Christians are finding their mutual commitments and areas of agreement are much stronger than the areas of disagreement. They have decided to build on those strengths and the impact has been encouraging. For eight years the church leaders have been meeting together every week to pray, resulting in a number of initiatives.
4. In the spirit of a good conversation, I would invite readers to continue the discussion about God with me by letter or over the web – see the blog http://buildingabetterworld. typepad.com.

*we sort out the mess we are in?* Yet the intrinsically important thing is not what we say, but the way in which we say it. In my own journey of faith, a crucial moment was the one at which I began to talk *to* rather than *about* God. That choice remains yours. God may answer us powerfully, or he may silently walk with us.

There are many people who have experienced prayer being clearly answered, and many who have found God to be, at times, a silent companion. C.S. Lewis, one of the most popular writers of the 20th century, encountered long periods of depression and confusion in his own Christian journey, precipitated by the death of his wife and the apparent inability of God to help him or hear him. Yet Lewis knew that God was there, and continued to trust that his *faith* would carry him through the darkness and loneliness of bereavement. In my own life, I have found times at which God's presence and power have been particularly close – in the sudden death of my father and the attendant heartbreak I simply *knew* that God was carrying me, helping me and keeping me going. I conducted his funeral and knew God's help and support as I walked before the coffin, conducted the service and pronounced the committal at the graveside. Yet in the months that followed his death I wondered where God had gone. I knew that he was real, but I could not feel his strength and presence. It was only when I realized that one day all of the questions I had of God would be answered, and that on that day the answers would no longer matter, that I was able to move forward again in my faith. *But the struggles are as important as the victories in my faith.* A conversation is supposed to contain both the good and the bad, the happy and the heartbroken.

Christian faith begins and ends with such a conversation. It is an unending conversation. It encompasses an awareness of our own weaknesses, mistakes and failings as well as the ultimate recognition that God, through Jesus Christ, has made a way for all things to be put right. It is not a conversation that is only open to the sure, to the convinced and to the morally pure. Rather, it is a conversation that allows us to grow, develop, change and mature. Right back in Chapter 1 as we were beginning this journey together, I described myself as a 'tainted, broken, cracked and often failing follower' of Jesus Christ. I carry on a conversation with him on a daily, sometimes hourly basis and I am content to know that slowly, gradually I am contributing to building a better world through my relationship with God. I am contributing practically and personally.

Practical in the sense that the conversation leads to action on my part. As I reflect and pray and allow myself to be centred on what God wants me to do I find that my priorities are changed. The focus of my life springs from my faith, and that in turn shapes the commitments and decisions that I make. I can then decide which meetings I should attend and which I should not. Which projects I can support and which I cannot. The aims and objectives of Faithworks, the movement I lead, are shaped by the faith that its members share. Faith has very practical implications not just for what I 'do' in my vocation but also the way my private life is lived. Our conversations and relationships with God mean that as a family our decisions are shaped in an atmosphere of faith and trust. Each day my wife, our four children and I pray together. We talk about our day and think about the things that we have done. The way we handle our money, our time and our possessions is shaped by our faith. Our faith shapes the way we treat each other and how we use our home. There is no area of my life that lies beyond the orbit of my faith.

Recently we decided that we needed to move home. The decision to move, and working out where we should look to re-settle the family was shaped by an ongoing conversation with God as a family. Where would be best to look for a new house? What kind of community did we want to be part of? What should we do about schools? What about the sort of house that we needed? Many of these decisions can be made without reference to God, but for us, God shapes these decisions. Because of our faith, we wanted to live in an area of social need. We wanted a home that was going to be large enough not just for the family we have, but a place where we could welcome strangers and those in need. We wanted to be part of a community that was trying to move forward and address the needs in the area. We also wanted a home that was in an urban area, but close to travel links because of the large amount of travelling and speaking that I do. When it came to the children, we talked to them and prayed with them about what they wanted out of a school and it became clear that they wanted to go to a state school, not a private one and they wanted to go to schools that were attended by other children in the area. Yet they also wanted to go to schools where they could contribute something, not just get something. The result was that we moved to Reading and live in an area of the town that faces real social and material challenges. The children attend the local schools, but that means that the three youngest are part of the local Roman Catholic primary school. The oldest, Matthew, is attending a school which has faced a very chequered academic record in the past but is beginning to improve. We are part of a Christian community in the town that is really trying to serve the local people and I have become involved in a number of town-wide initiatives that are aimed at helping and serving the marginalized and vulnerable. My wife is working as a Nurse Practitioner in a nearby surgery and able to serve those with whom she works and is finding connections and opportunities to make a difference in the lives of others every day. All of this has been shaped by our ongoing relationship with God.

So a conversation with God is not one that leads to theorizing alone. It leads to action, to changed behaviour. Otherwise the conversation is not true. My contribution is personal because I am being made a better person through it; the change is not just happening 'out there'. By being a conversationalist with God the change I want to see 'out there' in the world is first taking place 'inside' me. In the deepest, most prejudiced parts of my heart and life God is changing me and in so doing he is enabling me to be part of the solution in the world rather than just part of the problem.

It would have been easy for us as a family to decide we wanted to live in a nicer area with less social need, to send our children to good schools and to do what we want with our money, our time and our other resources. I have to say that the temptation to make decisions purely based on what I want lives with me all the time. Yet *because* of my ongoing conversation with God, I am constantly reminded that my priorities get out of sync with the priorities God has for me. My tendency to do things that benefit me – drive a fancy sports car, have lots of money in the bank, live in a very self-satisfying way, etc. – are challenged and changed by my faith. The result is the decisions that I make are changed because I am changed by my faith. My outlook is changed by my faith and that changes the way, I live. It is not always about me.

So to begin a conversation with God is to begin to allow our thoughts, our actions, our ambitions and our intentions to be shaped by him. It is to be open to the possibility of God changing us and changing the world through us. It is to consider relationally the implications of a God at work in the world through his people. It is to take the example, teaching and life of Jesus seriously. It is to acknowledge that he is at work in our lives already, which leads us to the next question.

We may need to change our thinking a little and recognize that this may just be the finest hour of the Christian community, if we handle it correctly. The pressures of post-modernity may well have given us a fresh opportunity to be the people and the community that we were born to be. Every community needs a centre. Christian community has its centre in Christ. Like him, we must become people who are open, welcoming, relevant and credible. We must take his life, example and teaching seriously. Perhaps we must take him more seriously than we have ever done before, for we can't afford not to.[5]

# 4. Find our fit in the world

What role do we believe Christian faith has in our world, and therefore *the* world? Is it a source of good or a source of bad? Are there ways in which we think that our understanding of this faith and its relevance have been changed in the time we have had together through this book? Is it possible that Christian spirituality has a positive contribution to make to our life and to society? Where does faith fit in our lives? Where do we fit in the world?

---

5. The theologian, Walter Brueggemann, is also right in asserting that it is both the teaching *and* the example of Jesus that is so challenging. 'If anything, his teachings were more radical than his actions, for his teachings played out the implications of the harsh challenge and radical transformation at which his actions hinted.' *The Prophetic Imagination* (Philadelphia: Fortress Press, 1978), p. 103.

## Three views of where faith fits

There are probably three main options from which we will make our choice. The first is the model that we see on mainland Europe. Here, Christian faith has been all but removed from the public square. The only way in which it impacts policy and society is through personal convictions. Christian faith is seen as a personal choice with no consequences on public policy or public life other than those afforded it by the holder. In fact, some would go even further and suggest that it is dangerous for Christian faith to be allowed any place in the public square.

The second option can be seen in some elements of the US conservative evangelical[6] world. Here Christian faith is often seen to support one particular view, or position, *en masse*. In the US context such mass support has created the impression that Christian faith is right wing and conservative both socially and politically. This approach leads to the conviction that there is a 'Christian' position on everything and that it is the duty of the follower of Christ to adopt that position. This can lead to the view that the Christian position is more motivated by a desire for political power and control than transformation. Thus it is variously termed as 'the religious right' or the 'moral majority'. It is exemplified in the words of Jerry Falwell in the run-up to the 2004 American Presidential election:

> It is the responsibility of every political conservative, every evangelical Christian, every pro-life Catholic, every traditional Jew, every Reagan Democrat, and everyone in between to get serious about reelecting President Bush.[7]

---

6. Here the term 'evangelical' is being used to describe what I refer to in Chapter 1 as 'Religious fundamentalism' but of a specifically Christian variety. I actually disagree with that use of the word quite strongly, as evangelical Christians contribute a great deal of good to society. For a fuller discussion around this theme, take a look at the website of the Evangelical Alliance in the UK, led by Joel Edwards. See www.eauk.org for a more balanced representation of evangelical Christians.

7. Jerry Falwell, *The New York Times*, 16 July 2004.

It is probably important to note that the idea that every single follower of Christ in the US thinks the same way, votes the same way and has the same moral view of every issue is just a little over-simplified! As I have said already, caricaturing a view may be easier for many people, but it is neither helpful nor accurate. There are some incredible stories of socially progressive followers of Christ in the US who are seeking to change the perception of the Church and Christian spirituality.

The third option is one that might just be emerging in the US and is certainly already present in the UK. The faith we hold is still a personal affair, but it has public consequences.[8] In it, our worldview is shaped by our faith and there is space and recognition in public life that faith matters. This distinctive approach argues that faith and its implications are vitally important for the world we live in. The point I am making is that this option forces us to take Christian faith and values seriously, but at the same time it holds us accountable for them. Christian faith shapes the way we view poverty, the environment, war, the media, human rights, terrorism and financial responsibility. Such faith leads us to engagement, partnership, dialogue and openness.

## 5. Keep involved

Christian spirituality has a home in many political domains. We must remember that. Christian faith is not owned by the Conservative party or the Republicans with their strong emphasis on family values and the need for respect. Nor is it the exclusive domain of the Labour party or the Democrats with their heightened emphasis on the poor and the marginalized and sense of social justice. Christian convictions cannot be tied solely to the Liberal Democrats, with their commitment to individual freedom and liberty, either. The political parties in the United Kingdom and the US present followers of Christ with two kinds of policies, ones that we can wholeheartedly endorse, and ones that we

---

8. For a fuller unpacking of this idea, see *God's Politics* by Jim Wallis.

cannot. The trick for us is working out what role our faith has in our social and political decisions. Should our faith and our politics be separated? Most of us know the old adage, to avoid confrontation – *Never talk about religion and politics*. Well, is it true? I've tried to overcome that myth in this book – because it doesn't work.

## Left or right?

Jim Wallis spoke at the Faithworks conference in November 2005. His book, *God's Politics* has been referred to on a couple of occasions throughout this book. He makes the point that Christian faith cannot simply be completely left wing or right wing politically. If that's true – the right don't get it and the left get it wrong – then our political decisions become even more important. The policies we support, the decisions we make, are vital to the health of our society. Politics is about values. How we treat people – how we educate them, care for them, live with them, protect them and house them. All of these 'political' decisions must flow first from how we understand people. How we understand people flows from how we understand the world. And how we understand the world flows from how we view God. Whether we like it or not, politics and faith are tied together. So if that is true, why do different Christians vote for different parties?

Jim is a strong social commentator. He's also a Democrat. Chuck Colson, the founder of Prison Fellowship, is also a strong social commentator and a Christian – he is a Republican. In the UK Tony Blair is a Christian and a member of the Labour party, but Alistair Burt is a Christian and a member of the Conservative party. Some people think that we should have a Christian political party, believing that it is possible for all Christians to have the same political views. I strongly disagree.

## Common ground

We need followers of Christ with strong faith in all political parties. Jim Wallis makes a lot of sense when he talks about poverty, but so does Chuck Colson when he talks about protecting vulnerable families and social cohesion.

Tony Blair and Alistair Burt both make sense. They both have strong views, and they are allowed to disagree. Our politics are not only shaped by our faith, they are also shaped by our experiences, personalities and preferences. While followers of Christ are committed to the cause of the poor, the strengthening of the family and the upholding of clear Christian values we disagree on how we believe we achieve those things. To suggest that all people of faith should have the same political opinion or vote for the same party simplifies the argument and ignores the diversity of those who have faith. Holding to a Christian spirituality does not equate with monochrome personality and opinion. A system where all followers of Christ voted for the same party would be both predictable and rather boring!

Against the big canvas of our faith, we have a responsibility to work out how we think the world can be changed to be a better place. Some Christians think that lower taxes enable a spirit of generosity in society. Others think that higher taxes ensure that the rich support the poor. We don't have to kill each other to prove a point! That simple illustration does show that we should think through how the world might become a better place, however.

I'm glad we don't have an American style of political engagement in the UK, but I would like to see some of the political activism of Christians in the US mirrored in the UK. I don't think our churches should vote *en masse* for the same party. I'm also glad we don't have a Continental style, where faith is pushed into the closet and politics is in public. We have a third way, where our faith shapes our view and we then make decisions politically based on our faith, our convictions and our preferences. That's good. Followers of Christ can become too dogmatic in politics just as we can be too dogmatic in church! When we start to talk as if the only political view a Christian can hold is the one that we share, we are in danger of making fools of ourselves and a mockery of our faith.

If politics is just about power, winning an argument and getting the limelight then we are in serious trouble. If the only form of political engagement open to us is one of criticism, argument and attack, we are in a mess. But that is only what we allow politics to be about if we don't take our own responsibilities seriously. The Christian standpoint should be one of dialogue, discussion, mutual learning and understanding and finding a working consensus. Democracy is not just about how we vote, it is about how we live.

God has given us intelligence, wisdom, discernment, free will and the ability to do something about the world. We should use all of them wisely. Saying that politics is just about voting is like saying that life is just about breathing or that an engine is just about oil. Politics, like faith, affects everything we say and everything we do. That is why it is impossible to separate our faith from public life. Britain needs faith in public life because faith in public life makes Britain a safer, fairer, stronger country and a greater democracy.

A privatized faith that has no impact on the world in which we live and the society we are part of, seems to me to be rather useless. A faith that connects us with the world, however, will be the most transforming motivation imaginable. It leads to a robust engagement with the deep challenges of our communities and a willingness to seek a better way of doing things. It does not demand that everyone believes the same things as we do, but it looks to share expertise, experience and resources with those who share our values. Such an approach allows us to be distinctive in our own spirituality, to be clear about what motivates us, without imposing our views on other people. It creates a space for people of all faiths and people of none to work together to build a better world and allows for unity without uniformity. It might just be the only way that religious fundamentalism and extremism can be overcome.

## 6. Build collaboration

The challenge then becomes to acknowledge that we are not the ultimate source or bringer of change and hope – God is. This is a diminishing of our own sense of self-importance that brings about a greater understanding of our own significance. We are *not* the one that must make everything work – God is. I am convinced that behind every act of compassion, grace and love the world has ever seen, lies the compassion, grace and love of God. I am more than aware that such a statement will cause consternation to many. Those of no faith and those of other faiths may well feel their temperatures rising as they read these words. To them, I am patronizing and offensive. My belief is this, whether or not we ever acknowledge God as the source of our kindness and compassion will not change the fact that he is that source. Christian spirituality does not remove our individuality; it allows each of us to be the person we were always meant to be. It does not demand allegiance to God, it invites it. It does not force us to believe, it leaves room for us to do so. Yet at the same time God inhabits our acts of love and our words of kindness. He uses them to change the world. He works with us not without us.

Some will be up ahead of us on the path, others way behind us. Some will even be just about where we are. Wherever we, or they for that matter, are, we are heading in the same direction. As we take the claims and example of Jesus seriously we must also learn how we relate to others who do not share our faith, but do share our values.

The world will not be changed by the Church alone. It cannot be. There are parts of our world, whole sections of it, where there is no Christian presence. Are we to suggest that these parts of the world should be forgotten? Are we to force them to become 'Christianized'? Or is there another way? I think there is. I think there are a common set of values and commitments that we have explored together that have their source and inspiration in Christian spirituality. God invites all those who hold such commitments – to human dignity, justice, servantheartedness, community, inclusion and diversity, holism, participation, hope and his presence in the world – to journey together, to work together and to weep together. He invites us to see him in one another. He doesn't just invite us to travel together, he longs for it. It is the only way that we can build a better world.

## Learning to sing a different song

So moving forward involves six steps:

1. Recognizing that change is possible.
2. Exploring our spirituality.
3. Moving beyond debate.
4. Finding our fit in the world.
5. Keeping involved.
6. Building collaboration.

As we do these things, we will create a greater momentum for change in the world. We can build a better world, but we can only do it together. In Chapter 1, I asked whether or not we could connect the lyrics of our lives with the melody that flows from Christian spirituality. Let me finish with that same analogy.

I'm pretty convinced that many within the Christian Church believe that the Church itself is the only thing that will change the world. In that sense, they see themselves as *the* orchestra and *the* choir. For them, the leaders of the Church are the conductors. I don't agree. The orchestra and singers that will change the world are made up of many different people, from different backgrounds religiously, socially, ethnically, politically and geographically – people like us. We each have a distinctive instrument to play and a specific vocal sound to contribute – touching on every sphere of life and every area of need. We each belong in a particular section of the orchestra and will play best when we find our place. Followers of Christ are part of the orchestra and part of the choir. Many will be in the same section, but not all. We are hidden in different sections too.

The conductor of this orchestra is not some abstract notion of God; it is not some nebulous force or power – he is an 'almost unseen' Person. Those who know the music and the lyrics have a clear understanding of who that Conductor is. The lyric longs for a better world – it is a lament because of how things are and a cry for what can be. The tune that is played is the melody of the principles of justice, goodness, mercy and hope. As it is played and sung, the audience is changed and they themselves become members of the orchestra itself. They join the choir. This song, this music is growing in strength and intensity. It is unstoppable. Finally, when the orchestra has played, and the choir has sung, there is a pause and the Conductor steps from the shadows and all those who have played will recognize his face and realize that he is the One they have spent their lives looking for. Whatever the background or ideas of those of us who play, we will realize that the Justice, Goodness, Mercy and Hope we have sought is standing before us, and his name is Jesus. Some will not realize it until that moment, though. Others, his followers, will smile, because they knew it was he that was conducting their lives. They felt him in every note they played. Without him the orchestra could never have played and the song could never have been sung. But *because* of him and *only* because of him, the world has been made a better place.

The challenge for those who are followers of Christ is to take our place in the orchestra, but not to dominate it. We must allow people to find their place too, and when asked, we must share the excitement and good news of the identity of the Conductor. However, we must allow people to take their place. We must not force them to play our tune. God within them will bring the music to their memories. Perhaps it is we who must learn to hear it? Those of us who are already followers of Christ must learn the art of making music with people who are different. We must recognize and celebrate the contribution to a better world of those who know the tune, but do not know the Conductor – yet. Their contribution is vital if the melody is to sound as beautiful as it can. We must learn to play the tune *together*.

Yet there are additional quavers in *this* song that are found nowhere else. Christian faith offers hope, forgiveness and a fresh start for all. It reaches out to anyone who will embrace God. The unique notes of Christian faith include such things as the opportunity to have *an individual* relationship with God and the wonderful experience of forgiveness of our own failings and shortcomings. Commitment to Christ as the ultimate expression of God and the only way to truly know the reality of who and what God is cannot be sacrificed because it is difficult. Our allegiance must remain to him. His birth, life, death, resurrection and promised return are all vital lyrics in this song. They make sense of life and death. They give hope and offer comfort. They provide a pathway through suffering. The melody includes the recognition that the world can only be made better as we ourselves are changed and transformed. Our responsibility is not just to *do* things to make the world a better place, it is to be *made* a better person ourselves through faith in Christ – and that is one of the greatest contributions that we can make to building a better world. All this is found in Christian faith.

Those of us who have faith in Christ must learn to celebrate the notes that others play and the words that others sing, and sing them with all our heart. At the same time, however, we might need to recognize that we can be guilty of getting stuck on just one part of the song. Salvation – the ultimate transformation and rescuing of all things by God through us – has many key components. Personal embracing of Christian faith is clearly vital and that can only happen through a relationship with Christ, but we must not become stuck there. There are notes of societal change, community transformation, environmental renewal, the resetting of political power and the redistribution of wealth which are also part of this wonderful melody. Those of us who already follow Christ find as many new notes and as many startling lyrics in this song as those who have not yet embraced God or felt his embrace. We must be open to that possibility.

For those who are part of the orchestra but do not yet know the Conductor, the challenge is to play the tune together *and* to explore why it sounds so *right*. How is it that people from such diverse backgrounds holding such different ideas can *know* the same tune? How is it that our contribution fits so perfectly with that of someone we have never met? Where does the *affinity* with the other singers and musicians come from? Certainly it springs from the love of the music and the enjoyment of playing and singing – but there is more to it than that. This music has a commonality, it has a sense of unity within it. There is only one answer – that the same Composer has written the whole score. He knows every note, understands every nuance and celebrates every musician. He knows that every single player and singer must work together if the melody is to be heard in all its beauty and power. He knows the melody, not only because he wrote it, but because he *is the melody*.

*The cost for each of us is great ... but worth it*

All of us must recognize the cost involved in being part of the orchestra and the choir. It is a cost that is lifelong. This is not an easy tune to play! Many will misunderstand our reasons for playing it. Not everyone in the audience will like what they hear. Some might even try to silence us. Following our leader inevitably leads us to a place of pain as well as a place of joy. There is a cross for each who would join the choir or pick up an instrument. As we play, we enter into the suffering and pain of the world as Jesus did. Our contribution to making the world a better place is one that will cause us heartache and pain. We, like Christ, will feel a deep and searing pain as we see the injustice and the suffering and the inequalities around us. However, we can look to his death and resurrection as the finale that we will join. He has made the ultimate contribution to building a better world – the cross and resurrection of Jesus Christ spring from a life of sacrifice and commitment. His whole life is a stake in the ground for hope. That stake in the ground is our inspiration, our source and ultimately provides for our transformation. For those reasons, we must not forget the cost of building a better world to God himself, and the cost to us. This melody has melancholy and lament as well as air and celebration. We play and sing both – it can be no other way.

So the challenge is to build a better world. It is to play our part, to make a difference, to take our place. But it is to do so, knowing that we are part of something bigger, something better than we ever thought possible. It is to look beyond ourselves, beyond others and catch a glimpse of a Conductor, to join the music we have been humming for years.

Looking around the orchestra of our lives, we will catch glimpses of others who are playing the same tune. We might be surprised at those we see. Yet if we can find the members of this orchestra, if we can welcome new members to the choir, surely that is better? There is always room for one more person. Our sound can be enriched and our tone made so much better by working *with* others rather than against them. As each of us puts down this book, or passes it on to someone else to read, perhaps the time for tuning is over; maybe the rehearsals have ended. Is it possible that now is the moment? As we reflect on what we have read, perhaps in the quiet we will hear the footsteps of Someone who is taking the stage. The Conductor's form is just recognizable, but in the silence of anticipation, we hear the gentle tap of a baton on a music stand. The melody is rising in your heart, the words are forming in our minds. We are about to begin. . .

# Postscript –
# Just us or justice?
# A word to the
# Christian
# community

I began this book aiming it at the millions of people who have supported the Make Poverty History campaign in the UK and the ONE campaign in the US. However, I want to take a few moments to talk directly with those who already see themselves as followers of Christ and as part of the Church.

This year has certainly seen the press reporting the massive momentum behind these initiatives. Millions of people have worn the white wristbands that show public support for the call to end injustice and make poverty a thing of the past. Like the Jubilee Campaign a few years ago, this campaign for justice for the world's poorest people has captured the hearts and the imaginations of millions of people across the UK and tens of millions across the world. In the words of Nelson Mandela, 'Sometimes it falls upon a generation to be great. You can be that generation ... Poverty is not natural, it is man made ... it can be overcome.' Live8 concerts were held in London, Berlin, Paris, Rome and Philadelphia in early July, and as 2005 unfolded the campaign garnered a great deal more publicity and steam as the G8 summit approached. Amongst the many people supporting the campaign I am also aware that there were a huge number of Christians. That can only be welcomed. It seems the Church is discovering again the reality that it is not 'just us' that matter, but instead that justice is very much on God's heart. In the growth of the movement to Make Poverty History, the Church is also rediscovering God's heart and our mission in the world.

## A biblical agenda for a post-modern age

Ask most people in Britain today to name some of the things that the Church should be involved in and you'll hear a common set of answers. Our society expects the Church to speak out on behalf of the poor. In fact a survey a few years ago by the Evangelical Alliance of the UK[1] showed exactly that. People in Britain *want* the Church to speak out on issues of injustice. They want to hear us call for help for the poor and the unsupported. There is a challenge in this call, though. For a very long time the Church has become known for its stance on 'traditional' moral issues such as abortion, euthanasia, sexuality and protection of the family. Of course we must continue to make the case for the sanctity of marriage and of life. If we do not do so, we fail in our biblical responsibilities. I feel as passionately about the sanctity of the unborn child and the vulnerable adult as I do about the poor and the marginalized. However, the challenge is to allow our morality to shape our views of justice[2] as well. When was the last time you heard a sermon on a passage of Scripture such as Amos 5 or Micah 6? The Church – and that means you and me as well as everyone else who belongs to the body of Christ – must make sure that we are following a biblical agenda for the world in which we live. That means that we must not create a notion of God which is western European, consumerist and happens to have the same

1. For more information see www.eauk.org.
2. I also think there is a valid argument that the issues I have listed here can be legitimately seen as issues of justice.

preferences and soap-boxes as we do. It is amazing, don't you think, that we hear so little preaching and challenge about how we spend our money, whether we shop ethically, what we do with our time and the way we invest our pensions but so much preaching and challenge about the need for morality and values to be pushed up the agenda for British society. We should not be silent about the issues that matter deeply to us – because they matter so much we should speak out. But we need to discover the broader biblical agenda that we have always been called to follow. That agenda forces us to stand with the excluded, the poor, the oppressed and the marginalized. We do not stand neutral, we stand with them because God stands with them. Once we grasp the nettle of engaging with people, everything starts to change.

## Changing the way we do things

Church becomes more authentically a set of relationships centred around Christ. We maintain the distinctives of being people who worship and love God and serve him individually and together, but we become a community that has a central purpose that can be articulated in two ways, both of which are encapsulated in the great command of the Lord Jesus himself. *We love the Lord our God with all our heart, mind, soul and strength and we love our neighbour as we love ourselves.* Just because we know this amazing commandment doesn't mean we can treat it lightly. In fact, the old adage is true: familiarity breeds contempt – or at the very least indifference. As Christians we have a clear mandate – to love God and to serve people with everything that is in us. Anything less is a pale reflection of biblical Christianity. You may not be surprised to know that from time to time I am accused of having abandoned the true Gospel in favour of a social Gospel. I'm told that the job of the Church is simply to preach the Word!

The Evangelical Alliance in the UK has become the facilitator of a collaborative approach to addressing the issues of social challenge and transformation in the UK. The Alltogether initiative is an attempt to draw together a wide range of people from different backgrounds to begin to address the issues that we need to consider and act upon in the UK. They have taken the bold step of giving this initiative away. By doing this, the Evangelical Alliance has shown it is committed to a collaborative approach to social transformation and are seeking to act as facilitators of genuine dialogue and partnership. I believe this could have a huge impact on the way in which members of the Christian community relate to one another and I am excited to be part of it.[3]

## Not ashamed of the Gospel

My response is simple – the Gospel was never just words! It has never been about shouting at society or at individuals. The Gospel is about words and deeds. It is about being like Jesus to the people we live with, work with and share this planet with. It's about having God's heart for people. Did Jesus only use words? Well, ask the man born blind, the woman with the issue of blood, the people at the wedding at Cana, the thousands he fed before delivering the Sermon on the Mount. Ask Lazarus or Jairus or the widow of Tain if Jesus only used words. Jesus not only spoke the truth – he was the Truth. When he touched people, Truth touched them. When he healed them, it was Truth, Grace and Love that reached into their hearts and made a difference. Jesus himself reminds us that every time we give someone a cup of cold water in his name, we have demonstrated the heart of God and somehow 'shared' the Gospel with them.

The Apostle Paul was not ashamed of the Gospel – and neither should we be. If we reduce the Gospel down to a three-minute prayer after a twenty-minute sermon in an hour-long service once a week we have missed the point. The Gospel that Paul was proud of was the message that God had reconciled the world to himself through his Son, the Lord Jesus. It was that the Kingdom of God had broken into the fallen world of first-century Palestine and that

3. Again, for more information see www.eauk.org or the Alltogether website, www.altogether.org.

it would never stop advancing. It was that sin had been dealt with, that God had made a way for people to have hope. It was that things do not have to be the same because God working through his Spirit and his people is making all things new. The Good News is that God is at work in the world and drawing people out of sin, pain, despair and hopelessness. That Gospel affects the way we view the world.

We must not be ashamed of speaking the truth. But we must not avoid being the truth as well. As you read these words, what you do matters as much as what you say. How your church behaves is a true indication of what your church stands for. You do not need to find a new agenda for the church to be 'successful'. You need to go back to the biblical agenda – to act justly, love mercy and walk humbly before your God. Let those simple truths shape the way you live as an individual, as part of a family and as a member of the community.

It has never been 'just us' that mattered – we need to rediscover justice.

## Appendix: What are the key ingredients for an effective Christian Social Movement[4]

Over the past 150 years or so, Christian movements for social change have come and gone. A few have stayed. Two of the most remarkable have been the Young Men's Christian Association and the Salvation Army. These two groups continue to have massive influence for good not only across the United Kingdom, but across the world. They are touching and changing the lives of thousands of people every day in pragmatic and in spiritual ways. But why have a Christian Social Movement at all, and what makes such a movement effective? Is such a thing worth trying?

## Why have a Christian Social Movement – building the Kingdom of God

The reason for Christian Social Movements is the Kingdom of God. The motivation behind working for transformation in the world is both deeply theological and sociological. Theological because the core mission of the Church is to be the central agent through which God brings hope and change to the world. Sociological because society is made up of individuals and can only change as individuals within it are changed. Far from being monolithic and isolated, the Church is called to be the greatest change-bringer the world has ever known – nothing short of the transformation of the world! Ultimately, Christian conviction pushes its adherents out of the comfort zones of our own believing communities into a world that is desperately in need. Those of us who claim to be followers of Christ are participants in the greatest 'paradigm shift' the world has ever seen. We are a community of

4. The contents of this appendix were originally published in *Faithworks News*, March 2006. The appendix is focused on the Christian components of a social movement and although it repeats a quote from Charles Finney that I use in the main body of *Building a Better World* I believe the appendix has a number of important messages for those who are part of a Christian Social Movement.

people whose lives are being transformed by God, agents of transformation in the world. This is not a new idea at all. In fact the 19th-century evangelical revivalist, Charles Finney, believed passionately in a church that changed the world. In his now famous book *Lectures on Revival,* he wrote:

> The Great Business of the Church is to reform the world . . . the church of Christ was originally formed to be a body of reformers. The very profession of Christianity implies the profession and virtually an oath to do all that can be done for the universal reformation of the world.[5]

Christian communities that have locked themselves away from the political and social challenges of their contemporary culture are irrelevant. They may be settled and surviving, but they will eventually choke to death because true mission is to the Church what air is to the human body. Separation from society leads to stagnation and death for Christian communities. What, then, are the key ingredients of a Christian Social Movement? There are many vital elements but I want to highlight just three.

## Committed to Christ

Jesus Christ must stand at the heart of any effective Christian Social Movement. Without him, the movement's ethos, values and distinctiveness will be lost. The greatest dangers that Christian Social Movements face are the seduction of power, influence and popularity. When these things become more important than our commitment to Christ, we lose not only our effectiveness, but also our heart. When the centrality of Christ is denied in a movement, the very source of greatest influence is also denied. However, it is the whole person of Christ who must remain at the heart of a Christian movement, not just one group's interpretation of him.

The strongest Christian Social Movements are motivated by the

5. Finney, *Lectures on Revival,* pp. 18–19.

whole life and example of Christ. There is plenty of room for a breadth of understanding of Jesus and his ministry. Catholics can stand alongside Evangelicals who can stand alongside Orthodox. Pentecostals and Pietists can share this mission with Anabaptists and Charismatics. Each can and should bring their distinct perspectives of the person and ministry of the Son of God. The Political Jesus *is* the Suffering Saviour. The Compassionate Christ *is* the Holistic Healer. The birth, life, death and resurrection, with their rich tapestry of meanings and implications, must be allowed to be interwoven to create the strong, unbreakable fabric of spiritual, social and political transformation. To have a many-faceted Christ clearly at our heart is to allow ourselves to be strong at the centre, making us open and completely inclusive at the edge. At the heart of the American Civil Rights Movement of the 1960s there was quite a diversity of opinion around Christ – from liberal to conservative, black to white, liberator to suffering God. The fact remained, however, that the whole person of Jesus stood at the centre of that movement. He was the embodiment of freedom to those oppressed and of hope to those long discouraged. Yet he was not narrowed by one theology or held down by one denominational view. The same must be true of a modern Christian Social Movement. Christ is the One from whom we gain our inspiration, our identity and our vision. We must never apologize for him because he has never apologized for us.

## Focused on people

Secondly, Christian Social Movements must be focused on people. We may want to see change in policies, procedures and legislation, but they are not our ultimate aim or focus. As we seek to bring his Kingdom in, we seek to do so one life at a time. We are the ones who wade into the river to help those who are drowning. Of course, we also feel strongly compelled to stop people falling into the river in the first place. We do not seek changes in the law for no reason, however. We seek them because we are focused on people. Christian Social Movements do not see people on different tiers. We do not see some people as more important than others. Instead, we recognize that every human being is made in the image of God and therefore on an equal footing with us and all other people. A human person is entitled to respect, dignity, acceptance and love. This clear focus enables us to serve, not from a position of power and privilege, but instead from a place of equality and grace. When we engage in the service of others, we do not 'condescend' to serve. Rather than reaching down to someone else, we reach across to them because we recognize that they are of equal value to God as we are. When a movement gives up its focus on people for a focus on programmes it becomes nothing more than another organization. We may use statistics, but we never treat people as just statistics.

This is a crucial component of the Christian Social Movement because it celebrates the dignity of life wherever it is found and it levels the place of service. We learn from St Francis of Assisi who saw an act of compassion to the poor as a sacrament – a place where the veil between heaven and earth is truly thin and we meet God in a special and sacred way. People are never simply the objects of our charity; instead they are individuals with names, hopes, aspirations and struggles just like us. They cry like us and they laugh like us because they are the same as us. They don't just need our charity, they need God's justice and mercy in the same way as we do. If losing Christ's centrality means we lose our inspiration, then losing people as our focus means we will lose our purpose. We cannot afford to lose either.

## Delivered through the Church

Lastly, effective Christian Social Movements are committed to delivery through the Church because the Church is at the heart of the Kingdom. Catching a vision of the Church as *the* agent of change and redemption in society means that our congregations, committees and communities will never be the same again. Strong and effective Christian communities are birthed by this expectancy. One of the greatest mistakes the Church makes is when we begin to function for our own sake rather than for the sake of others. There is no sense in which the Church is called to self-preservation. Instead, every denomination, network and new church stream is called to be part of a massive movement of transformation – spiritual, social and political – that changes the world. We need a Christian Social Movement because without one we have failed in the greatest commission and commandment of the Scriptures – to love God with all our hearts and our neighbours as ourselves.

This commitment to church is not a commitment to one form of church, though! Indeed to be most effective many forms of church must be embraced. From the innovative and new to the traditional and established, the Church becomes a gloriously diverse vehicle of transformation. A Christian Social Movement that is not committed to the local church is like a river without a riverbed or an arrow without a bow. Too often in their developments, historic movements have seen themselves as apart from the Church. The truth is that every person involved in a Christian Social Movement is also part of the Church. The movement is the melody played out through the instrument of the Church. To forget that is to create a tuneless song played desperately out of key.

## Conclusion

I am convinced that Faithworks is *part* of but not the *entirety* of a Christian Social Movement. Only as Christian movements allow their own agendas to be submitted to the agenda of God's Kingdom in favour of a common cause and higher goal will we see lasting transformation of the world. The time for narrow-mindedness, exclusive deals and defensive doctrinal posturing has long since past. Unity without a purpose is both unbiblical and unnecessary. I do not need to agree with all of your theology in order to work with you as a fellow Christian, nor do I need you to agree with all of my thinking for you to work with me. We will disagree about many things, but if we can put Jesus at the centre, people first and remain committed to the body of Christ, then we have all the ground that we need for unity and collaboration. There is too much to be done for us to waste time arguing about the finer points of our theology. The world needs us, Christ calls us and we must answer – together. Only then will we build a better world for ourselves and for our children.

# More information about Faithworks

To find about more about any of the work of Faithworks including details contained in this section, please contact:

Faithworks
115 Southwark Bridge Road
London SE1 0AX

Tel: 020 7450 9000

Email: info@faithworks.info

Web: www.faithworks.info

## Purpose of the Faithworks Movement

The Faithworks Movement exists to see transformation of individuals and communities through Christ. It has three main objectives:

- To inspire, resource and equip individual Christians and every local church to develop its role at the hub of its community, serving unconditionally.
- To challenge and change the public perception of the Church by engaging with both media and government.
- To encourage partnership across churches and other groups to avoid unnecessary competition and build collaboration.

The Movement was founded by eleven partner organizations and these organizations continue to play an important role in its development. Faithworks has a lead partner in the Oasis Trust, which provides the majority of Faithworks financial support, supplies staff and office space and seeks to provide models of inclusive activity as examples of good practice for the wider Movement.

## Resources

Faithworks have made a number of resources available that aim to help individuals, churches and organizations. These include:

- *Networks and support* aimed at Christian engagement with the community at a local, regional, national and international level. This involves either the formation of new networks or support of existing networks.
- *Training and consultancy* that helps local projects and churches to run professional projects; be equipped and trained for engagement with the community and wider society and work effectively in partnership.
- *Published materials* such as books, manuals and guides that help projects deal with the principles and pragmatics of engaging with the community, working with other voluntary and faith groups and with the government and other statutory bodies.
- *Web-based resources* including a website, articles, virtual networks and regular updates on issues such as funding, key opportunities, policy developments and events.
- *Working groups* that focus on particular areas of engagement within society so that projects and churches can be best equipped in addressing key issues such as education, healthcare, housing and crime prevention.
- *National leadership* on behalf of those involved in the Faithworks Movement to engage with the Church, the government, the media and wider society on issues of social action, social justice and inclusion.

- *Theological reflection* around the issue of the core message and mission of the Church.
- *Speakers* for local, regional, national and international events who aim to inspire, challenge and encourage the Church to engage with the community unconditionally.

## Getting involved in the Faithworks Movement

There are lots of ways of getting involved in the Faithworks Movement. All of them involve people becoming *activists* not just observers. Here are just a few:

### Membership and supporters

Faithworks membership is free and will ensure you are kept in touch with the Faithworks Movement. Sign up today online at www.faithworks.info/join. Membership enables you to have access to the resources and information that Faithworks distributes. It also ensures that you are able to connect with people who have the same commitments, passions and struggles as you do. Membership of Faithworks is about more than putting your name on an email list. As a member of Faithworks, you become part of a growing movement across the world that is seeking to see radical and lasting change in communities through Christ.

Faithworks is almost entirely financed by voluntary donations – and in order for the movement to develop and grow it needs *supporters* in the form of individuals, churches and organizations willing to commit to regular financial and prayer support. This is a straightforward process that enables better strategic planning of the development of the movement.

### Partnership

Faithworks is actively encouraging partnership built around four fundamental areas – purpose, principles, priorities and processes.

# Appendix

Formal partnership in the Faithworks Movement is open to all Christian churches, organizations, networks and individuals through signing the Faithworks Charter and Partnership Agreement. The Charter sets out commitments and principles for service delivery and the Partnership agreement sets outs how partnership in the movement works.

## Faithworks Affiliates

One form of partnership is affiliation. You can officially affiliate your church, Christian community project or organization to Faithworks. This is an opportunity to belong to a recognized nationwide network, which will aid your negotiations with statutory agencies and increase your funding potential. As a Faithworks Affiliate you will receive an official certificate recognizing your Faithworks affiliation and the right to use the Faithworks registered logo. In addition to all the benefits of personal membership, you also have access to free downloads of the growing number of practical tools produced by Faithworks to assist your church, organization or project in developing effective work in the local community. We also offer Affiliate discounts on consultancy and training and we are constantly reviewing how best we can serve you. To affiliate to Faithworks visit www.faithworks.info.

## Networks

### Local networks

You can partner with Faithworks as a local network of churches, projects and organizations across a town, county or region. If you are starting a network, we ask you to ensure that the churches and projects that join your network individually affiliate with Faithworks nationally, entitling them to all the benefits of affiliation. However, beyond these simple principles we recognize that each local network will be unique and established in a way that is appropriate for the local community and that flexibility should be encouraged in the formation or running of networks. It may be that you are already involved in an effective network. This whole network can join the Faithworks Movement. Where there is a strong local network, there is no need to start another one, but there may well be added value in the network and Faithworks learning from each other and working together. The name of a local network is not the most important thing – what matters is that it is working unconditionally to serve the local community and is committed to good working principles, practices and partnership.

As a Faithworks Local Network, you will be given the opportunity to host Faithworks regional events to inspire and resource your members and beyond. If you want it, your local network will receive a specially designed Faithworks logo, which will include the name of the town, region or area in which you operate for use on all literature and publicity that you produce in relation to your Faithworks affiliated activity.

**Regional networks**

Faithworks is committed to effective regional working. Working with a regional leader and a small number of people who make up a voluntary advisory group in each of the twelve regions in the UK, Faithworks seeks to serve the Church in partnership with networks such as the Churches Regional Network, the YMCA and others. The aims of regional working are:

- To ensure the best informed development of local networks.
- To highlight particular regional issues and appropriate responses.
- To develop the most effective models for a particular region.
- To allow for regional diversity while ensuring a sense of unity and purpose across the whole movement.
- To enable effective access to regional resources, funding and specialisms.
- To be a first point of contact for existing Faithworks members and partners in the region.

## National and international networks

Faithworks is committed to working in partnership with other organizations that have a national presence. This includes major organizations such as the Shaftesbury Society, the Evangelical Alliance and Churches Together in Britain and Ireland and all of the denominations. All of these organizations, including Faithworks, must recognize that if we expect local churches and projects to work together, then we must also model partnership and joined-up thinking and networking. For that reason, Faithworks is committed to ongoing dialogue, shared resources and joint working on a national and international level. There are a number of areas where this can be improved – from work with government through to the delivery of training and resources. Faithworks is keen to explore national and international networking with as many groups and organizations as possible to avoid duplication and strengthen delivery to local projects and churches and communities.

## Where is Faithworks going?

As the Faithworks Movement moves forward, it is important to know where we are going. Faithworks also seeks to model authentic Christian community. By 2012, Faithworks seeks to see the following developments in its work in the United Kingdom:

- Provide regular information to 250,000 individual members.
- Serve 300 Faithworks Local Networks in the UK.
- Serve Regional Networks in every area of the UK.
- Act as a facilitator of national co-operation and joint working for Christians engaged in social action in the UK by providing space, time and opportunity for discussion, dialogue, joint working and successful partnership and by working in partnership with as many national denominations and organizations as possible.
- Facilitate the provision of excellent resources to members of the Faithworks Movement at every level.

- Continue to articulate and work toward the key objectives of the movement by developing specific advisory working groups to develop recommendations and support around the following key areas of activity:
  - Healthcare
  - Education
  - Housing
  - Crime reduction
  - Environment
  - Children and young people
  - Citizenship
  - Family and relationship support
  - Financial management
  - Community development.
- The articulation and development of a new approach to the role of Faith in Public life built on commonly held values while allowing for theological diversity known as Distinctive Faith.
- See 50,000 individuals contribute financially to the movement on a monthly basis with a resultant income from individuals of £1 million.
- See organizational, denominational and national financial support of the movement develop and grow.

The transformation of individuals, communities and society as a whole is possible. Faithworks is committed to providing the best network possible across the UK and beyond to enable that transformation to take place. While there is one community that suffers from exclusion or one church that does not open its arms to embrace those whom God has made, the mission God gave to his people is not complete. The task may be daunting, and the challenges great, but as we work together, we can and will see our world changed – we can build a better world, but we can only do it together.

# Bibliography

Bell, Rob, *Velvet Elvis: Repainting the Christian Faith* (Grand Rapids: Zondervan, 2005).

Brueggemann, Walter, *The Prophetic Imagination* (Philadelphia: Fortress Press, 1978).

Brykczynska, Gosia, ed., *Caring: The Compassion and Wisdom of Nursing* (London: Arnold, 1996).

Burke, John, *No Perfect People Allowed: Creating a Come as You Are Culture in the Church* (Grand Rapids: Zondervan, 2005).

Bush, George W. and Hughes, Karen, *A Charge To Keep* (New York: William Morrow, 1999).

Chalke, Steve, *Trust: A Radical Manifesto* (Milton Keynes: Authentic, 2004).

Chalke, Steve and Watkis, Anthony, *Intelligent Church: A Journey toward Christ Centered Community* (Grand Rapids: Zondervan, 2006).

Chester, Tim, *Good News to the Poor: The Gospel and Social Action* (Leicester: IVP, 2003).

Claiborne, Shane, *The Irresistible Revolution: Living as an Ordinary Radical* (Grand Rapids: Zondervan, 2005).

Colson, Charles and Pearson, Nancy, *How Now Shall We Live* (London: HarperCollins, 1999).

Conder, Tim, *The Church in Transition: The Journey of Existing Churches into the Emerging Culture* (Grand Rapids: Zondervan, 2005).

Edwards, Joel, *Hope, Respect and Trust* (Milton Keynes: Authentic, 2004).

Ellsberg, Robert, ed., *Gandhi on Christianity* (Maryknoll, NY: Orbis Books, 1991).

Falsani, Cathleen, 'Bono's American Prayer', *Christianity Today* 47, no. 3 (2003).

# Bibliography

Finney, Charles, *Lectures on Revival* (Minneapolis: Bethany House Publishers, 1988).

Hoekema, Anthony A., *Created in God's Image* (Grand Rapids: Eerdmans, 1986).

McGrath, Alistair, *Christian Spirituality* (Malden, MA: Blackwell, 1999).

McLaren, Brian, *Generous Orthodoxy* (Grand Rapids: Zondervan 2004).

Mounce, William D., *The Analytical Lexicon to the Greek New Testament* (Michigan: Zondervan, 1993).

Murray-Williams, Stuart, *Post-Christendom: Church and Mission in a Strange New World* (Milton Keynes: Authentic, 2004).

Rahner, Karl, *Theological Investigations* (London: Darton, Longman and Todd, 1966).

Schluter, Michael and Ashcroft, John, eds., *Jubilee Manifesto: A Framework, Agenda and Strategy for Christian Social Reform* (Leicester: IVP, 2005).

Stockman, Steven, *The Spiritual Journey of U2* (Orlando: Relevant Media Group Inc., 2005).

Toynbee, Polly, *Hard Work: Life in Low-pay Britain* (London: Bloomsbury, 2003).

VanGemeren, Willem A., ed., *New International Dictionary of Old Testament*, vol. I *Theology* (Carlisle: Paternoster Press, 1997).

Wallis, Jim, *The Call to Conversion* (Abingdon: Marston Books, 2006).

—— *God's Politics: Why the Right Gets it Wrong and the Left Doesn't Get it* (New York: HarperCollins, 2005).

—— *Faithworks* (London: SPCK, 2000).

Yancey, Philip, *Rumors of Another World* (Grand Rapids: Zondervan, 2003).